"As a fellow theologian mom, [illegible] Coolman. She's been an exam [illegible] both in the work of theology and in the vocation of parenting. So I am thrilled and grateful to be able to endorse her new book. Readers will find in Coolman a wise and gracious guide eager to help other parents with their vital work of 'apprenticing children to love.' Church leaders will find numerous insights into how best to support parents and children. There are a lot of books about parenting on the market—and I've read most of them. But I think *Parenting* is uniquely thoughtful, inclusive, and peaceable. It is a resource I recommend to anyone who cares about children, parents, and the vocation of child-rearing in God's kingdom."

—**Emily Hunter McGowin**, Wheaton College

"I literally learned parenting and theology on Holly's couch, and I'm so glad her wisdom is now available in this book, which is different from any other parenting book you've encountered because it's first about who God is."

—**Beth Felker Jones**, Northern Seminary; author
of *Practicing Christian Doctrine*

"Holly Taylor Coolman offers people of faith and indeed all people a beautiful perspective on the challenges and rewards of parenting. I am particularly grateful for her wise words about the complexity of parenting today, whether through fostering, adopting, giving birth, or other forms of relationship (grandparenting, parenting from distance, etc.). Far from offering distant ideals, Coolman writes from the thick of her own experience. This book is real and will lift readers to see the vocation of forming children into adults as shot through with grace, even in the hardest times. Read, and then share this book with parents and those involved in family ministries!"

—**Tim Muldoon**, Boston College; coauthor
of *The Discerning Parent*

"I simply adored this book. In *Parenting*, Coolman has created an invaluable resource for any parent in any season of life. Who doesn't want to love their children better? To know them more fully? To have more peace and joy in their home? Coolman writes like a friend who's been there, bringing a lifetime of wisdom and scholarship. She doesn't sugarcoat the challenges of parenting even as she encourages her reader to delight in the task."

—**Anna Keating,** author of *The Catholic Catalogue: A Field Guide to the Daily Acts That Make Up a Catholic Life*

"Parenting is both a gift from God and a wilderness. I can't think of a better guide to receiving well the gift and navigating the wilderness than Holly Taylor Coolman, who writes out of her deep faith, theological understanding, and profound experience. Reading this book was like having a long conversation with a very wise friend about things that matter most. I look forward to recommending this book to parents in my congregation."

—**L. Roger Owens,** Pittsburgh Theological Seminary

PARENTING

THE COMPLEX AND BEAUTIFUL VOCATION OF RAISING CHILDREN

HOLLY TAYLOR COOLMAN

Baker Academic
a division of Baker Publishing Group
Grand Rapids, Michigan

Visit www.bakeracademic.com/professors
to access discussion and reflection
questions for this book.

© 2024 by Holly T. Coolman

Published by Baker Academic
a division of Baker Publishing Group
Grand Rapids, Michigan
www.bakeracademic.com

Printed in the United States of America

All rights reserved. No part of this publication may be reproduced, stored in a retrieval system, or transmitted in any form or by any means—for example, electronic, photocopy, recording—without the prior written permission of the publisher. The only exception is brief quotations in printed reviews.

Library of Congress Cataloging-in-Publication Data
Names: Coolman, Holly Taylor, 1967– author.
Title: Parenting : the complex and beautiful vocation of raising children / Holly Taylor Coolman.
Description: Grand Rapids, Michigan : Baker Academic, a division of Baker Publishing Group, [2024] | Series: Pastoring for life : theological wisdom for ministering well | Includes bibliographical references and index.
Identifiers: LCCN 2023020248 | ISBN 9781540961495 (paperback) | ISBN 9781540967237 (casebound) | ISBN 9781493437962 (ebook) | ISBN 9781493437979 (pdf)
Subjects: LCSH: Parenting—Religious aspects—Christianity. | Parenting—Biblical teaching. | Christian life.
Classification: LCC BV4529 .C5985 2024 | DDC 248.8/45—dc23/eng/20230706
LC record available at https://lccn.loc.gov/2023020248

Scripture quotations are from the *New American Bible with Revised New Testament and Revised Psalms* © 1991, 1986, 1970 Confraternity of Christian Doctrine, Washington, DC, and are used by permission of the copyright owner. All rights reserved.

In chapter 1, the excerpts from "Prayers of the Faithful" are used by permission from the English translation of *The Order of Baptism of Children* © 2017, International Commission on English in the Liturgy Corporation. All rights reserved.

Baker Publishing Group publications use paper produced from sustainable forestry practices and post-consumer waste whenever possible.

24 25 26 27 28 29 30   7 6 5 4 3 2 1

For my dad, who asked me questions—
and listened to my answers

For my mom, who looked
for ways to make things beautiful

For Boyd, a parenting partner
who excels in a thousand ways

Contents

Acknowledgments

A book with so big a topic owes much to many. Thanks go to my parents and my sisters, and also to my grandparents, whom I remembered often as I wrote. The friends who have been a village for my husband and me as we parented know who they are; I love you all. In our family, there will always be a special place of honor for our children's birth parents and birth families. I am grateful to God for writing us into your story and writing you into ours. Kelly and Tania both gave me crucial encouragement to take some thoughts about parenting and make them into a book, and Anna Moseley Gissing, Melisa Blok, and everyone at Baker Academic did so much to make those thoughts as good as they could be and to help them find readers. Particular thanks go to Jason Byassee, who gave me the initial invitation to write and whose patient, gentle encouragement and editorial wisdom was essential. Old friends are the best friends, and Jason is one of the best of the best. Finally, I have to acknowledge my children, who have so far survived my attempts to figure out parenting and who, in ways big and small, make me proud every day.

Introduction

I remember clearly the precise moment I became a parent. In some ways, a familiar script unfolded. My husband and I rushed to the hospital. Friends and family waited anxiously for a phone call that would deliver the good news. And then, it happened. I was handed a gorgeous baby, rosy with dark hair. I had waited and hoped, and now here she was, a perfect little human being, entrusted to our care.

In other ways, I felt as if I were outside looking in, watching a scene I had never expected. Only a few moments earlier, I had held my daughter's birth mother's hand as this beautiful baby was born. This little girl was now nestled in my arms, but at that moment I suddenly felt flummoxed. "Well, hello there," I remember thinking. "You're the baby, and . . . I guess I'll be . . . the mom." It was enormous.

I am not the only one to experience the transition to parenting in this way. And if that first moment of parenthood does not create the sense of being in over one's head, it is all but guaranteed that some later moment will. To become a parent is to be entrusted with something infinitely precious: a human life. Parents take up a work of intense companionship and tender, relentless formation unlike any other.

At this particular historical moment, even more, particular challenges come into play. "It takes a village to raise a child," says the oft-quoted African proverb. For parents in the developed world, though, that village can be very difficult to find. Realities like the industrial revolution and the appearance of the automobile have re-made family life. "Work" now usually means traveling some distance away from home and being gone for ten to twelve hours at a time. Working from home is a welcome alternative for some, but it can also highlight even more sharply the fact that the work involved just does not mix well with the care of children. Parents face a difficult set of choices. They can join that world of work; they can focus instead on their children, isolated from other adults and from all kinds of work beyond routine housework and childcare; or they can try to combine the two, usually with complex childcare plans or by trying to hide away in front of a computer screen.

Living in the wake of industrialization also means that nuclear families (consisting only of parents and their children) often exist in isolation from others. They may live far away from extended family and communities. Indeed, they may lack meaningful, long-term social connections of any kind. Perhaps partly as a result of these pressures, even these smaller family units struggle to come together and to *stay* together. Many are sorting it out as single parents, often with remarkably little help. In the midst of all this, many parents are seeking connection and support wherever they can find it.

As I was typing the first paragraph above, I heard the ding of an incoming text message, which said this: "We are in a parenting crisis and need support. I wonder whether you might consider listening. If you can do this, please give me a call." This friend did the right thing. In an unnerving moment, she reached out for help. She and I were able to talk for almost an hour about a sudden challenge with a teenager, a situation that was both confusing and frightening, and that required her to make important decisions quickly. The value of having a name and a number, of having a reliable listening ear, in a situation like that is impossible to overestimate. And how much better would it be if conversations about children and parenting were just a routine part of life lived in community? Leisurely consideration of all the challenges of family—big and small—is not a luxury but a necessity if parents are to thrive. The presence of a supportive community is the essential foundation for this work.

For parents of faith, the stakes of parenting are only higher. They are more likely to see their work as something more than chance or even choice—to see their lives with their children as a calling. And part of this calling is usually a deeply held desire to hand on the faith, something that rests at the center of all they do as parents. But parents of faith can see the waves of secularization around them. The statistics are not in their favor if they have the goal of seeing children and grandchildren make faith their own.

Not long ago I spoke with a man in his seventies, someone deeply committed to his faith and deeply devoted to his work in the church. The sadness was palpable as he spoke of the way that first one, then two, and finally all four of his adult children have left behind the practice of their faith. It is increasingly common that even parents who have given their best efforts must watch as the children walk away.

Our language marks the growing sense of challenge involved in raising children. The word "parenting" only first appeared in the twentieth century. The prevalence of its occurrence spiraled upward in the 1970s, '80s, and '90s, and the number of books published on the topic exploded during the same time. Today, books on parenting are everywhere. Somehow, a fundamental human task has come to feel like an overwhelming task, something that must be pursued with tremendous levels of intentionality. Time and care and thought must be given—not simply to the care of children but to *figuring out* the care of children. "Parenting," it is now assumed, requires a great deal.

This is not to say, of course, that parenting is simply a matter of feeling overwhelmed. Family life continues to be a source of unique and deep joy for a lot of parents. Many will report that it is the most rewarding work they have done. Accompanying other human beings in this whole-person sort of way, over a lifetime, is perhaps the most fundamental form of risk—and of embodied hope—possible.

And even with the challenges, many parents have high hopes. They feel the joy of this responsibility, and they want to do it well. They want their children to be safe and well-fed. They want to provide the right enriching activities, carefree time spent together as a family, and warm memories. They step forward in optimism.

The Christian tradition offers a profound analogy for this decision: God is often described as a parent. In Hosea 11, the Lord says:

> Yet it was I who taught Ephraim to walk,
>   who took them in my arms;
>   but they did not know that I cared for them.
> I drew them with human cords,
>   with bands of love;
> I fostered them like those
>   who raise an infant to their cheeks;
> I bent down to feed them. (vv. 3–4)

The God described here is a tender, doting parent, and the passage suggests that parents, as they love and teach and care for their children, are imitating God. The day-to-day may look like just a succession of small, silly moments, whether wonderful or difficult or tedious. Ultimately, though, mothers and fathers are doing nothing less than participating in the form of Love that grounds all of reality.

The gift of themselves that parents must give in this undertaking is both intimate and transcendent. Perhaps that's why it is so deeply connected to faith. To take up something so personal and also so much larger than myself is to step into the fundamental questions of spirituality: "Who am I, anyway?," "What is the good to which I am called?," and "How can I find the strength to do it?" Becoming a parent, amid it all, brings an invitation to reconsider and renew one's own faith.

And here, too, the Christian tradition offers invaluable resources. Parents can find insight and reminders of God's grace available to both them and their children. They can be reminded of the dignity and importance of what they are doing. They can be reassured that—although the task is great—help is available. In an important way, in the face of current trends toward isolation, they can be invited into a village.

The church, after all, is something more than just a gathering like any other. It is a communion. The earliest Christians are described in the second chapter of Acts as "devot[ing] themselves to meeting together" (v. 46) and as selling possessions in order to provide for the needs of others in the community. The metaphor most often used by Jesus to describe the church, strikingly, is a family. At a moment when what many parents need most is a form of an extended family, or a village, this metaphor offers a profound possibility.

What would it look like to invite parents into shared sorrow, shared joy, shared meals, shared life? What would it look like to meet parents in the hard places, the beautiful places, in every place?

This volume explores these questions and invites readers to step into the work of parenting—and of accompanying parents—with creativity and courage, considering what might be involved in supporting, empowering, blessing, and challenging them as they live out the vocation of raising their children. It will suggest that there is, in fact, much that can be offered and done.

My reflections here are deeply shaped by my own experience. For more than twenty-five years, I have been parenting while also studying and teaching theology, first as a Protestant and now as a Catholic. In that time, my husband and I together have adopted five children, the first three as infants and the youngest two as tweens. We have stepped into the day-to-day realities of householding, including community, loss, trauma, discovery, attachment, and celebration. We have lived in several different communities, and we have sent our children to private schools and public schools, as well as homeschooling all of them at one time or another. Through it all we have learned not only about our children's strengths and needs but about our own. We have come to see the ways in which not only they but we live in vulnerability and radical dependency on others. We know even better now how completely unprepared we were, back on that first day in the hospital.

But in a very real sense, no parent is prepared. To be a parent *is* to be in over your head, knowing that you have been entrusted with something bigger and more important than you can accomplish on your own. At the same time, there is no richer work. With the power of grace, with the strength of solidarity, it can be an experience of the deepest joy.

New Parents

A new baby involves a world of preparation. "Painting the nursery" is a powerful symbolic act: parents are making room, making things ready. Choosing the right soothing shade for the walls is an embodied way to say, "We are longing to meet you, little one, and we have so many plans—not only for this space but for a larger reality in which you are wrapped in love." The long strokes of painting the walls give a place to put the hope.

As we prepared for our own first child, our simple nursery held so much: a crib and dresser that had been my own when I was an infant; a new bookcase painted to match; and small, framed prints of characters from Beatrix Potter's *Peter Rabbit*. As our baby was expected through adoption, there were added layers of uncertainty, but we felt the same sort of wonder that all new parents feel: "Soon, there will be a new *baby* in this room!"

A waiting this intense is a sort of little Advent. Most parents do not, of course, await a divine child. We know, however, that Christ's entering-in hallows everything it touches. In the Incarnation, God is related to all that is by a mysterious new personal indwelling. God is conceived in the womb of Mary, and suddenly, at the moment of conception, all of the tiniest human lives—and, indeed, the whole material world itself—become in a new way the dwelling place of the Most High. In taking up human life in this way, not only is God revealed to human beings but the deepest truth of human existence is revealed, including the beauty and dignity of its quietest moments. New babies, and the preparation made for them, are part of this remarkable reality—and are the focus of one of the church's most important liturgical seasons. New parents become privileged observers of, and participants in, this mystery at the center of the faith.

Not only that. A simpler, more ancient reality exists here as well. To paint a nursery—or to engage in any of the countless tasks on a new parent's to-do list—is a particular kind of waiting. New parents are ready for the work of hospitality, of preparing for and welcoming. Hospitality is everywhere in the Christian tradition. "Exercise hospitality," says Romans 12:13. "Be hospitable to one another without complaining," readers are instructed in 1 Peter 4:9. These simple commands are rooted in traditions like the description of the fasting that God desires, described in Isaiah 58:7: "Is it not sharing your bread with the hungry, bringing the afflicted and the homeless into your house; clothing the naked when you see them, and not turning your back on your own flesh?" Hospitality is a central part of living as God's people.

All of this makes sense when we see how the hospitality that we offer, including the hospitality that parents offer to their children, is connected to some of the most profound theological themes.

On the one hand, we recall God's own deep and fundamental hospitality, a hospitality expressed above all in creation. It may seem odd to think of it in this way, but the reality of creation is just this: God, who exists independently, chooses freely to speak a world into existence and gives to creatures a true existence of their own. In a deep sense, God makes room and welcomes all that is not God. In everything that follows, this making-room continues. In the process of salvation, God treats human beings with generosity and courtesy, inviting them in, in a way that respects their free will. Parents have a unique possibility of participating in this reality, welcoming children and living hospitably in an echo of God's gracious welcome.

On the other hand, perhaps unexpectedly, we are also called to offer hospitality to God. What is perhaps the best-known icon in the world illustrates the point. The icon goes by the name of the scene it depicts directly: "The Hospitality of Abraham." Recalled here are the events of Genesis, when three mysterious visitors suddenly appear at

Abraham's tent. Abraham urges his wife, Sarah, to prepare a meal of the finest bread and meat to serve them, and once they have eaten, they deliver the unexpected promise that, although she is past child-bearing years, Sarah will give birth to a son. The icon depicts these three visitors at a table, but it also intends indirectly to symbolize the Trinity (who can, of course, never be directly depicted). The fundamental claim of the icon is a striking one: just as Abraham found these strangers at his door, we encounter God as a guest. In our own way, we are invited to make room, to welcome God in, to give the best we have. And so, a kind of circle: our children are not the Divine Child, but they arrive as he did, asking us not simply to paint the nursery but to stretch and reconfigure and to make room, often in ways we do not expect.

Ultimately, something unexpected happens. In the preparations they make, and the gesture of hospitality they prepare to extend, parents themselves are remade. A new baby makes new parents. These tiny people come not just with their many needs but with the power to draw adult caregivers into new ways of seeing themselves—and the world around them.

In this we see one more theological truth. In Scripture, the God who is exists before and beyond us—and yet calls all things into existence—is nonetheless named by the relationship to God's children. This God is the "God of Abraham," the "God of Sarah." So, too, with parents, who become "Ben's mom" or "Elizabeth's dad." A first baby does this in particularly profound ways, moving their parents for the very first time to see themselves and one another as "mother" or "father"—with everything that those names mean.

The lived experience of most parents rests in two feelings above all, and they are closely intertwined: a new sense of wonder and a new sense of responsibility. Painting the nursery—and all the other kinds of preparation—are really connected to both. Making official announcements, borrowing a crib, purchasing a new house, celebrating a baby shower: all the preparations in anticipation of a baby's arrival have a practical function. At the same time, they do something more: help parents feel that they will be ready for that remarkable moment when their child actually arrives, when they hold in their arms a human being who depends on them completely—a human being who will, from that moment on, have a firm hold on their hearts.

In the end, they can never be fully ready. Any parent leaving a hospital, stepping out and placing their tiny cargo into a car seat, knows this. The world suddenly seems bigger and more dangerous. It is a world they cannot control.

Some parents know this especially well, as they face very particular challenges in trying to move forward. For some, the expectation of a baby is, from the first moment, the cause of uncertainty or even fear: It is not the right time. Perhaps it is not even the "right" partner. Life is busy. Money is tight. These are real concerns, and some of them are serious.

What all parents need, though, is the same. They need others to come alongside them and to share in both their sense of awe and their sense of responsibility. They need friends, but ideally, they need even more: the sense that they are woven into a web of friends, a community. They need to know that they are not alone.

For the bulk of our children's growing-up years, our family has had the great privilege of living in an increasingly unusual location: a thriving neighborhood. We know families up and down the blocks surrounding us; we have several good friends to whose house we can walk for dinner; our children have attended school a block away from home. What this physical proximity has made possible is a network of community support. Casual get-togethers are a regular feature of neighborhood life. My husband and I both have jobs outside our home, but we also have friends who can pick up a child from school in a pinch. When a middle-of-the-night emergency happens (as they seem to happen to every family), we always know we have someone close by to call.

Not everyone is so lucky, of course. Part of what that means is that there are immense opportunities for, and challenges to, communities of faith. From the first moment of announcement, individuals and the community as a whole can step up to offer support to parents in many ways.

In the first place, and especially where it is particularly needed, church communities can assist new parents with immediate material needs. Developing a community tradition of baby showers is one way to do this. Individual members of the community can be encouraged to take responsibility for one another, to find out what parents need most. Concrete possibilities are everywhere—although the individualism of our culture means that people may need to take a firm hand. "Let us know if you need anything" is not nearly as helpful as "What can I bring you for dinner?" Other practical kinds of help include offering to sit with a baby while parents attend to other children or chores, providing housecleaning or a gift card for cleaning services, or even helping with laundry. Taking a load of sheets and towels and returning them clean and folded can be nothing less than a godsend for sleep-deprived parents.

Personal and emotional support can come at the same time. For parents who are not already surrounded with friends and family, there will be a powerful need for conversation and friendship. Checking in, telling stories, and connecting in various ways are not just "extras" for parents awaiting a new child; they are essential. This is a real test case of whether the community itself is healthy and functioning as it should, and of whether there are effective forms of pastoral care in place. Where these are found wanting, those in leadership have a helpful impetus for re-evaluation and improvement.

In our family, we saw a powerful example of this kind of support with one of our children's birth mothers. Unexpectedly pregnant as a college student, she faced an avalanche of challenges and decisions to be made. Choosing to place her baby for adoption answered some questions but also created a whole new set of tasks to complete and, of course, profound losses to grieve. Her church community accompanied her in more ways than one. They organized a baby shower with gifts that kept adoption in mind: frames for photos, keepsakes connected in various ways to birth and adoption, personal items for her that would foster a sense of care. Once the baby was born, all of us involved in the adoption were given a blessing and a send-off at a Sunday morning service. We left to begin parenting this child, knowing that his mother would not be left alone.

We have also benefitted from this kind of support. When our first child came home to us, my husband and I were both graduate students, as were many of our friends. Money was tight for all of us. But several people came together to organize a beautiful baby shower.

A neighbor knitted a blanket by hand. A friend managed to rescue an old rocking chair that was abandoned on the curb and repainted it so that it was ready for us when we arrived home. So many hours were spent rocking in that chair, and we still have it today.

What would it mean for all parents to welcome a child surrounded by this kind of care? When we recognize the importance of the task that parents undertake, how can individuals and communities of faith do anything *other* than commit to this task? It is communities of faith, after all, that are truly equipped to support parents in a holistic way: offering these material, psychological, and personal forms of support while also recognizing and honoring the deep spiritual truths at play.

Every new baby is a unique creation and a gift of God. Babies arrive as a blessing not only to their parents but to the whole church community. Babies and their parents need more than rocking chairs. They need to be prayed for and with. They need opportunities for instruction and reflection. They need the power and grace of the church's sacramental life.

From the earliest moments of a pregnancy, a new baby can be included in the prayers of the family and the community. Baby showers can include not only diapers and onesies but also gifts connected to faith: a first Bible, a Bible story book, a first rosary. If a baby's name has connections to Scripture or to one or more saints, then that can be a place to focus in gift-giving and prayer. Whether at a baby shower, gatherings of family or friends, or elsewhere, gifts can also include slips of paper with favorite Bible verses, prayer cards, quotations from favorite saints, and so on.

When one of my own godchildren was baptized, his mother and father asked friends, family, and godparents each to write a letter to the newly baptized. Years later, on his eighteenth birthday, all who had written these letters were invited to gather online and read them aloud. The letters of those who had passed away were read by others. This intensely beautiful event demonstrated a powerful way of remembering and reiterating the prayers that had followed him throughout his growing-up years.

Baptism itself, of course, is a central moment in the life of faith, and the baptism of a new baby is the paramount moment in which the church stands with new parents in welcoming their child. Catholic and Orthodox families are encouraged to baptize a child within a few weeks of birth; planning often begins before the baby is born. But whenever a child is baptized, the symbolism and spiritual realities are rich and deep. This rite of initiation into the church also tells us much about the realities of parenthood. Baptism is the sacrament of faith, but in the case of a baby, it is others who speak for a child unable to make a conscious act of faith. The child is then entrusted to those who have the solemn responsibility of nourishing that faith. We all rely on others to lead us into the realities of faith and even to speak for us when we are unable to do so. Both new babies and new parents need a community to step up and to surround them. They need all the forms of support already mentioned. They need a community who will pray for them in the way the Roman Catholic baptismal rite describes in the Prayers of the Faithful:

> "Give these children new birth in Baptism through the radiant divine mystery of your Death and Resurrection, and join them to your holy Church . . ."
>
> "Make them faithful disciples and witnesses to your Gospel through Baptism and Confirmation . . ."
>
> "Lead them through holiness of life to the joys of the heavenly Kingdom . . ."
>
> "Make their parents and godparents a shining example of the faith to these children . . ."
>
> "Keep their families always in your love."[1]

At the moment of baptism, the baby (and the baby's family) also serves the community in the beautiful way that it embodies this truth: none of us stands alone. None of us finds faith alone. What the baby and the baby's family need, we all need. These children, who in some sense belong to the whole community, remind us of our deep interconnection.

At the same time, baptism symbolizes and recognizes the dignity of both the child and her parents. As the baptized child is incorporated into the church and recognized as its newest member, it is striking that a son or daughter thus becomes, at the same time, a brother or sister. A baptism is joyful but never silly, and the underlying sobriety reminds us of all that is at stake.

When a child is baptized into Christ's death and resurrection, the paschal mystery itself is recalled, and those present participate in it anew. In this way, the demanding and blessed work of parenthood—and every part of human life—finds the unshakable foundation of its hope. The difficulties of parenthood cannot be avoided. In some cases, the vocation of parenthood will draw mothers and fathers directly into disappointment, confusion, and grief—into countless little deaths along the way.

Here at the very beginning, though, baptism can serve as a reminder that as crushing as these little deaths are, these children have *already* been taken up into a larger and deeper reality, where Love has the last word. As nerve-racking as the prospect of parenthood is, there is reason to remain grounded in hope. And in all the moments—sweet, exhausting, painful, mysterious—parents can be sustained by faith.

As they care for their children, parents, too, are folded into Love.

2

Beyond Birth

Other Ways of Welcoming Children

When we speak of families and parenting, we often think first of families formed in the most common way: a child or children who are born to, and raised by, their biological parents. There is nothing wrong with imagining this first. As an adoptive parent, I am keenly aware of blessings and advantages that are available to children who grow up in this way. Many of our families, however, are formed otherwise.

Significant numbers of children are raised in kinship care (in the care of extended family or with friends who are like extended family), in foster care, and sometimes by stepparents and/or adoptive families. In the US, approximately four million children—about one in twenty—live with one biological parent and a stepparent.

A growing number of kids (more than 2.5 million) are living with extended family and close friends, including about a million who are being raised by their grandparents. About 400,000 children currently live with foster parents, and about 250,000 children came to their families by adoption.[1] And beyond all these, extended family members and others can become folded into the household, whether for the short term or the long term. One of my children's friends has been staying at our house for the past several months. We would not describe her as "our child," but she is certainly a part of our household at present, and she has become part of our family story.

So how can we expand our imagination to include these families, and how should we understand their needs and gifts and their place in our communities?

We might begin by noting that families other than and beyond simple nuclear families occupy key moments in Christian Scripture and tradition. The story of Moses in Exodus 2, for example, commands our attention.

Moses is born in a moment of profound pain and uncertainty: his parents, along with all the Hebrews, are enslaved in Egypt. Of Moses's father, Amram, we learn very little. His mother, Jochebed, however, stands at the center of a remarkable drama. Even in slavery, the Israelites are growing in number and strength, and the pharaoh fears them. What if these slaves were to revolt and to support Egypt's enemies in war? As they seek to limit the Hebrews' strength and fruitfulness, Scripture says, the Egyptians are "making life bitter for them" (Exod. 1:14).

Egyptian cruelty is nowhere clearer than in an edict Pharoah delivers shortly before Moses's birth. Speaking to the midwives who assist Hebrew women in birth, he orders them to kill any male newborn before even handing them to their mothers. So for Moses and his mother, the situation is not just difficult but dangerous—intensely so.

The reaction of the midwives, however, is to defy Pharoah and to protect these baby boys. (Hebrew women, they insist to Pharoah, give birth too quickly for them to get there in time, and so they cannot carry out his order!) This is the first in a series of decisions that serve to protect Moses and deliver him to a new and expanded family situation. Once their actions allow Moses to be safely born, his mother hides him to keep him safe, until she can do so no longer. She then takes a papyrus basket (the Hebrew word is "ark," and it is the only time it is used other than the Noah story), waterproofs it with bitumen and pitch, and places it in the reeds along the banks of the Nile, hoping and praying. Moses's sister, Miriam, stays and waits and watches.

Then Pharaoh's daughter appears at this very spot along the Nile to bathe. (Should we not assume that Jochebed knew she would bathe there?) She sees the basket, sends a female slave to get it (perhaps a Hebrew herself?), and finds Moses inside. She recognizes that this is a Hebrew baby, and we can be sure that she is aware of the position her father has taken toward the Hebrews. The baby is crying, and she is moved by compassion. Here, Miriam steps out of the shadows and addresses Pharoah's daughter directly, asking whether she should get one of the Hebrew women to nurse the baby. Pharoah's daughter agrees, and thus Moses's own mother becomes his nurse, even as he enjoys the protection of Pharoah's daughter. It might even seem at this point as though Pharoah's daughter is nothing more than a protector for Moses.

The text goes on to add two crucial details. First, when he is older, Moses's mother brings him back to Pharoah's daughter and "he became her son" (Exod. 2:10). Second, it is Pharoah's daughter who gives the child his name, "Moses," because it means "to draw out," and she "drew him out of the water." Pharoah's daughter, then, becomes much more than simply a caretaker. She truly adopts Moses as a son.

None of this, however, means that Moses's Hebrew identity disappears. Even after he has reached adulthood, he remains in Pharoah's household, but he also identifies strongly with his own people, the Hebrews. Years later, he is described as happening upon the ugly scene of an Egyptian overseer beating a Hebrew slave. Feeling overwhelming solidarity with that slave, Moses reacts in impulsive anger and kills the cruel overseer. It is striking that Moses belongs to both his Egyptian and his Hebrew families—a fact that makes so much more poignant later confrontations with Pharoah, in which Moses conveys God's command that Pharoah release the Hebrews from bondage and let them go free.

Amid all the twists and turns of the story, one thing is clear: the families of the Bible are not always constituted in simple or straightforward ways. Moses is both truly a Hebrew and truly a son of Pharoah, and the complexity of his identity is precisely what prepares him for the work before him. In family situations that feel complex and challenging, we too can have hope that God is at work, and that it may be precisely from these situations that children are sent out prepared for whatever work it is to which God calls them.

We see some of the same themes in an even more central Christian narrative, that of Jesus himself. As Christians often recall in our Christmas celebrations, Mary is unwed when she conceives her child, a situation ripe with possibility for embarrassment and shame. And of course, the Christian affirmation of the virgin birth means that Joseph is not Jesus's biological father at all but rather an adoptive or foster father. If parents raising children not biologically their own feel awkward or challenged, if they feel out of place, they need only to begin by recalling that their family resembles the Holy Family itself in fundamental ways. If they worry about their children, or feel that they are at a disadvantage, they can remember that not only Moses but also Jesus himself was crucially prepared for the vocation that lay before him in a family that was different from most.

It is not only these narratives that remind us to look beyond biologically related families. The New Testament describes our own relationship to God as one of an adopted child to an adopted parent. Ephesians 1:4–5 says that God "chose us in him, before the foundation of the world, to be holy and without blemish before him. In love he destined us for adoption to himself through Jesus Christ, in accord with the favor of his will." The basic truth is not hard to grasp: we are not children of God simply "by nature" but because of God's gracious action to draw us in, to establish a relationship by which we are sons and daughters.

This is not just a marginal point. This imagery is so central to the New Testament that the late Anglican scholar J. I. Packer has written, "Our understanding of Christianity cannot be better than our grasp of adoption."[2]

Families in which parents care for children not biologically their own, and adoptive families in particular, can find in this central emphasis a deeply rooted kind of dignity. Adoption can be understood as an image of God's will and purpose for all of humanity. For the whole community, adoptive families in their midst can serve as a kind of icon of this truth.

For my own family, these kinds of reminders of the dignity of adoption have been life-giving. One of my sons, asked to write a paper on a biblical character, gravitated immediately to writing on Moses—in the first person. In the many situations in which we have felt that we were treated as if our family were second-best, remembering the place adoption holds in the Christian tradition has reminded us that our family has its own value and integrity, as well as a unique way of testifying to and embodying God's love and graciousness.

At the same time, it has become clearer and clearer to us that the lived experience of adoption involves difficulty and loss, especially loss for those who leave their family of origin in order to be adopted and for parents who lose the opportunity to be their children's everyday parents. When a mother or family hands their child over to new adoptive parents—even when that decision is made carefully and with love—trauma is involved, and it is sometimes a trauma that is only slowly unwound and fully experienced over time. Adoptive families that are formed may be deeply good. They may be places of welcome and joy, and an image of God's own love. The joy, however, does not simply erase the grief, and adoptive parents never simply replace birth parents.

Something analogous is true in other kinds of situations in which a child grows up apart from one or both biological parents. When a marriage ends in divorce, there are real losses to be grieved. A blended family may work hard and give children love, support, and stability, but the loss of having two parents married to one another and present together is real. Even in the best-case situations of divorce, when adults work together and children are prioritized, something has been lost.

Resistance to recognizing these losses sometimes grows out from good intentions: a desire to see the good in the new situation, or to support parents who are working—sometimes working very hard—to make that situation a success. The key here is that these desires for the flourishing of the new family, and recognition of all the good things that come out of it, can actually coexist with respect for ongoing loss. The task for the adults involved is to do the psychological and spiritual work to incorporate both, and thus to make space for the children involved to incorporate both as well.

Churches are especially tasked with the need to honor this complexity. Christians have a particular temptation to focus on divine providence and God's ongoing redemption of all things, and to imagine that these realities simply erase any sadness. In the Christian

tradition itself, though, we find profound resources to express that
sadness.

> Out of the depths I call to you, LORD;
>   Lord, hear my cry! (Ps. 130:1–2)

Even more to the point for those who are in a supporting role is the
instruction of Paul in Romans 12:15: "Weep with those who weep."

Not to suggest that this is simple. Children grow and change, and
they process the realities of their families in varying ways. Different
members of the same family may experience it differently. No formula
can be written for when and how joy and grief are combined. Knowing about these realities can move us to sensitivity. The question is,
How can we make a space for families in which all of the realities of
their lives are welcome?

If all parents can be imagined as offering a form of hospitality,
then it is also true that in these more complex kinds of family, there
are at least two additional kinds of hospitality that parents are called
to offer. First, parents must make space for their own feelings of
loss, as well as those of their children. In family life, where there is
already a swirl of emotions and day-to-day challenges, children need
an invitation to speak about such loss, and to know that their adult
caretakers will receive it with patience and tenderness.

Second—and potentially even more challenging—parents must
make space, in a sense, for those who are missing. For parents who
are divorced or widowed, this means honoring the absent parent
in whatever ways are possible, giving children avenues and rituals
to honor the missing parent, or simply refusing to engage in vit-
riol after a difficult divorce. For those raising nieces, nephews, or
grandchildren, and those who are foster or adoptive parents, the
challenges are somewhat different. The goal, however, is the same:
to make room for someone who is an integral part of their child's
identity and story.

These are not always easy demands. How much more, then, do
these families need a community that makes space for *them*? How
much more do they need a place where they are welcomed, nurtured,
and honored? As they are shown hospitality, these parents, in turn,

will be strengthened in their own vocation of hospitality. What sorts of actions, specifically, might that involve?

Above all, these families need simply to be remembered and considered. Their stories also need to be told in homilies and formation programs. Biological connection has its place, but it is not the only definition of family. The details of individual families' lives have to be treated with discretion, of course, but they can be invited to share those details where appropriate. Likewise, the openness of the Christian tradition to the sadness of loss needs to be included often in the story of faith that we unfold. There are occasions when this will be particularly obvious. Mother's Day and Father's Day, for example, if they are observed, are opportunities to recognize the many forms of motherhood and fatherhood.[3] Advent and Christmas are a time to remember the unusual form the Holy Family offers. This is a form of consideration that is most effective when wound through *every* aspect of community life.

Grandparents who are raising grandchildren, foster parents, and those who have adopted children coming from a background of trauma deserve special consideration. These are intensely demanding kinds of parenting. As is true of parents with new babies, practical kinds of help are especially needed here. These are situations where the larger community, and especially the church community, is called to lean in. One-time favors like dropping off a meal or providing children transportation to activities are good but even better is establishing a longer-term commitment to this kind of assistance and even to an informal extended-family sort of arrangement.

Churches can also be an invaluable place for foster parents and adoptive parents to find one another. Meeting their children's needs is done best in the context of community wisdom and support, and church community is a context well-suited for this connection, whether via informal friendships between families or more organized support groups. In a few remarkable cases, this kind of connection has blossomed into something bigger: a particularly "foster friendly" or "adoption friendly" faith community. Families have created networks that encourage others to undertake foster care or adoption, even if they might not have considered it otherwise. The possibilities for exchange of information and other kinds of mutual support are significant, and in a situation where they are honored and supported, families find that the sometimes daunting work of foster care and adoption are possible.

Before concluding this chapter, we should turn our attention to a particular situation: parents who are still living but are absent from their children's lives. This might be a father estranged from his children, a mother who placed a baby for adoption long ago, or a parent whose children were removed from their care by the state. We have already spoken about the need to honor and to remember these parents. It is important also to note that they *are* parents, even if their situation as parents is not what they might have hoped. These are often hidden parents. In some cases, friends around them do not know of their situation. And in some cases, almost no one knows about the child from whom they are separated. These are situations in which we must tread carefully, being sensitive to the details of each person's story. We would be naive to imagine that they have forgotten their child. Like other parents, they need a web of support, a place to tell their story, and a community in which they are seen. Notably, in its litany of heroes of faith, Hebrews 11 recalls Moses's birth parents: "By faith Moses was hidden by his parents for three months after his birth, because they saw that he was a beautiful child, and they were not afraid of the king's edict" (v. 23). As the narrative of Moses's eventful life unfolds, Jochebed and Amram fade into the background. We don't know what, if any, connection to Moses they continue to have. But they have played a part. As are all those in complex family situations, they are woven into something larger than themselves, something that God can take up into the purposes of Love.

3

Fostering Community, Within and Around

A strange thing happens for parents living out family life in the Christian tradition. Their children—the little people they are feeding and dressing and instructing—also become siblings when they recognize them as sisters and brothers in Christ. Particular roles are in place, of course, but this surprising connection reminds them that there is something bigger at work. The more this claim is unfolded and lived into, the more fully we can see the way that parents who build a family are also building a *community*. As they raise their children, parents are also providing the first opportunity for practicing community, for learning love and interdependence. This community is the one that will prepare the way for all the others to come.

The Christian tradition teaches us that human beings are meant for community. From the very start, the unfolding cadences of Genesis's creation account draw the reader's attention to this truth. One after another, various aspects of the emerging creation are recognized by God as good, right up to and including the creation of the first human being. Suddenly, however, there is one glaring exception: in Genesis, God sees that "it is not good for the man to be alone" (2:18). The animals have already been created, but they do not address this lack.

So God meets this crucial need, creating another human being whom the first immediately recognizes as a companion:

> This one, at last, is bone of my bones
> and flesh of my flesh. (2:23)

Many traditional societies are better than we are at recognizing this reality. In Africa, the Ubuntu tradition is captured in the saying: "A person is a person through other people."[1] Each person is a unique and profoundly valuable individual, but even as individuals, we only know ourselves—and in a fundamental sense we only come to *be* ourselves—through the mediation of relationship.

In all this, the family plays a uniquely important role. If human beings require rich, multilayered webs of connection to one another, then the family is the foundational place where this reality is first learned and lived. Above all, children arrive as dependent, and in the context of a family, this dependence is met and honored. Loving parents delight in giving their children what they need. In gestures as simple as a morning kiss, a hand that steadies a wobbly bicycle, or a shared meal, the family offers a place where commitment to one another and dependence on one another build a basic pattern of life. As children grow, they are then invited into this reality. The family home, when it works as it should, is a place where the sharing of resources establishes patterns of care and of generosity that last. In the long run, these patterns increase in intricacy and find full flower. Human beings are complex, and life is difficult. In a community of love and trust, this means that commitment and interdependence find full flower in a whole host of practices—practices that constitute the essentials of any community life: generosity, vulnerability, truth-telling.

Families are not intended to be simply launching pads for individuals to take up their own personalized, ambitious projects or to sit alone with their own sadness and heartbreak. Each individual within the family is called to be *for* the others.

For Christian parents, the family becomes a microcosm not only of a human community but, even more specifically, of a community that lives "in Christ." As early as the fifth century, Augustine refers to the family as a "domestic church," reminding us that a family rooted in faith is the most immediate, local embodiment of church. Imagining the family in this way opens up a whole host of ways to pursue family life.[2] The practical counsels of New Testament writings take on particular nuance when we consider them in the context of family: "Be kind to one another, compassionate, forgiving one another" (Eph. 4:32); "encourage one another, agree with one another, live in peace" (2 Cor. 13:11); "let us no longer judge one another, but rather resolve never to put a stumbling block or hindrance in the way of a brother" (Rom. 14:13).

Paul's references to the "body of Christ" also give new ways to understand interdependence and to remind us that all members of the family, although they operate with differing gifts and differing tasks, are nevertheless indispensable to one another. "The eye cannot say to the hand, 'I do not need you,'" Paul says in 1 Corinthians, "nor again the head to the feet, 'I do not need you.'" And then he goes on to add something crucial: "The parts of the body that seem to be weaker are all the more necessary, and those parts of the body that we consider less honorable we surround with greater honor" (vv. 21–23). To live as the church means not just connection but a special focus on those who are most needy or who are most likely to be overlooked in the broader world. Christian families, then, may honor and remember elders who have grown weak—not simply out of necessity but rather out of conviction that this care is essential to their very identity as Christians. Children who arrive with a disability are not just to be tolerated and accommodated but to be honored and prized. In the "body" that makes us family, such members have their own particularly important role to play. The long-term effects of practices such as these can also produce a habit of questioning: Who are those who are least honored? What perspective is required in order to see that they are actually deserving of special honor within our shared life?

All this is possible, as it is in the broader church, when family members are able to see one another not simply as companions but as God's own beloved. In his classic work *Life Together*, Dietrich Bonhoeffer puts the fundamental challenge this way: "God does not will that I should fashion the other person according to the image that seems good to me, that is, in my own image; rather in his very freedom from me God made this person in His image."[3] Parents naturally have high hopes for their children, and it is inevitable that they will form a sense of who their children are—or could be. It is easy to think of examples—"My child will be athletic"; "My child will value formal education." Bonhoeffer's words remind us that parents cannot allow that image to obscure the reality of *the person that the child is*. It is this person to whom parents are called to draw close, to accompany, to love. In the end, both challenge and profound freedom lie in this call.

When they can see one another rightly, family members are then called to love one another in a very particular way. The very heart of Christian love is that we love not as we have been loved by others but, rather, as Christ has loved us. In this way, family life can be more than just a tally sheet of debits and credits; it can be a place for the kind of love that God demonstrates, what the New Testament calls *agape*. This is favor that is in no sense earned; it comes only from the overflow of the one who offers love.

This is not to say that wrongs will never be addressed in family life. Life in the church requires relationships of reciprocity and accountability. The Gospel of Matthew offers key advice: "If you bring your gift to the altar, and there recall that your brother has anything against you, leave your gift there at the altar, go first and be reconciled with your brother, and then come and offer your gift" (5:23–24). This crucial principle is strikingly embodied in the kiss of peace that was part of ancient Christian liturgies and has now been revived in many places. That kiss—or its contemporary analogue, a hug or a handshake—is not intended primarily as a sign of simple friendliness but rather as an indication of the responsibility Christians have to address the wrongs committed among and between them. The kiss of peace happens *before* those present move to the sacrament of communion. This can be a significant, concrete teaching moment for parents.

So it is in the day-in, day-out of family life. Being family requires the work of peacemaking. Being a peacemaker, however, is not primarily a commitment to overlooking wrongs but a commitment to the hard and sometimes uncomfortable work of addressing them and seeking reconciliation with one another. The asking and giving of forgiveness is absolutely central in this regard and is something parents should prioritize as they foster family life. It is not uncommon for parents to ask children to apologize, but a deeper and richer set of habits may emerge when we think in terms of asking forgiveness. To ask forgiveness requires four things: (1) noting the wrong, (2) acknowledging harm to the other, (3) expressing our regret, and (4) indicating an intention to act differently. Even with small children, this formula can be captured in very simple ways. The most powerful strategy for instilling a practice of asking forgiveness in children will be parents who themselves ask forgiveness of their children when they err. How much formative effect is there in even a statement as simple as: "I'm sorry I spoke to you in an unkind way this morning. I know that might make you feel scared, and I'll try to speak more gently."

All of these ways of imagining family as an embodiment of church create deeper meaning in family life—and more specific goals for parents. Families are dedicated to many activities—educating children, providing food and shelter, creating safety and stability—but Christian parents are always being invited to see one another anew and to walk together in the light of God's love, God's presence, and God's purposes.

The way that parents exercise authority must also be shaped by this recognition. If their task is to shepherd children who are also brothers and sisters, parents will do so most effectively if their own authority is embedded in (and extends from) their own obedience to Christ, and if it follows Christ's own example. In particular, parents might note two aspects of Jesus's exercise of authority. First, it is always part of a larger commitment to the purposes of Love. Jesus is not demanding or self-seeking. His most striking displays of authority have to do with healing or with freeing those he loves from oppression. Second, he sees the particular person in front of him and acts in immediate response to that individual. We might think, for example, of Jesus's first miracle at the wedding at Cana. Turning water into wine could seem like nothing more than a party trick if it were done randomly. Readers can easily see the specific need to which Jesus is responding, though: hosts who have run out of wine may disappoint their guests, ruin the festivities, and be shamed before everyone. Even more, Jesus has a specific request from his mother, Mary, who seems to see the situation just as well. Parents are called to exercise authority in precisely this way: with care, precision, and love.

This undertaking is best led by the Holy Spirit. Parents must listen for the Spirit's leading and invite their children to do the same. Galatians 5:22–23 tells us in broad terms what this life will look like: it will be characterized by love, peace, and patience. Parents will lead not with harshness but with gentleness. Families, even when tired or challenged, will be characterized by an underlying joy. Pope Francis says it this way: Love is the center, but "against this backdrop of love so central to the Christian experience of marriage and the family, another virtue stands out, one often overlooked in our world of frenetic and superficial relationships. It is tenderness."[4]

Living family life in this way is a high calling, but again, it can be pursued in simple ways. Parents can ask children to do chores precisely as a community practice, or invite them to engage in small acts of kindness in quiet ways. Parents can look for ways to narrate situations as they appear naturally. "Your brother feels a little sad right now. Would you like to see if he wants a hug?" "Uh-oh, the baby dropped her toy. Can you get it for her?" Above all, parents can model the habits of life-giving community that they seek to foster in their children.

None of this is easy. So many obstacles can get in the way of living like this: everyday fatigue, concerns about health or money, challenges in marriage, frenetic schedules, and the constant distraction of various technologies. Extended family can bring its own set of painful challenges. Being present to one another is not easy, nor is the ultimate goal: to be "for" each other in a larger sense.

Sometimes the hard moments described above become something bigger and more painful, and some form of estrangement takes place. While this is always a tragedy, two possibilities are very real: people may find that family members pull away for reasons beyond their control, and (sometimes even more painful) people may take steps to limit or end contact with extended family members who harm them. No simple formula can make sense of these situations or tell families how to move forward. It is critical both for families and for those who accompany them to keep the ideal in view and also to seek life-giving ways forward when that ideal is not reality.

What do parents need in situations where the community of family has broken down? Above all, they need someone to listen and attend to them in all the details of their own stories. They need someone to honor the sadness and anger they feel, and to reassure them that they continue to be valuable and beloved. It may be that, in some cases, they need a prompting to seek or to grant forgiveness, but that must come from a voice they trust.

This building of community in family is always a work in progress. It is through trial and error, through a growth in the ability to hear the Spirit's voice, and through reliance on grace that families can move toward real and life-giving relationship. It is a task for a lifetime.

If individual nuclear families are called to live out community, they can do that well only if they themselves are surrounded and supported by community. In chapter 1 I spoke about the particular need that new parents have for support, but the fact is that all parents come to a moment when they realize they need a village.

Our family has had many such moments. I think of a time when I accidentally left an enormous pot of beans bubbling on the stove and went to bed. My husband and I woke in the early hours of the morning to an odd smell and opened our eyes to a house filled with smoke. Once our hearts stopped pounding, we realized that there was no fire after all; the smoke was coming directly from the pot. But everything in the house was saturated through and through with smoke. A few hours later, once the sun was up, I sent out an SOS, and my friends swung into action. One showed up with breakfast. Others came and hauled away basket after basket of smoke-filled clothes, bedding, and curtains, and took them home, returning them the next day freshly washed. I wept with gratitude and relief.

Or there was the afternoon when one of our sons tripped and fell headfirst onto a small and very sharp rock. My husband was at work, but my next-door neighbor appeared seconds after I called. She inspected the wound to confirm that a trip to the ER was required, and then took the wounded child's older brother home with her for some supper and a reassuring presence.

Emergencies like these may remind us of the need for community, but the need is there all the time. The situation of the industrialized West where two parents, or sometimes only one parent, takes on the work of raising children on their own is a highly unusual one. In most times and places, the most common situation for nuclear families is a life embedded in extended families, tribes, or villages.

The reasons for all this lie far beyond the control of individual families. Industrialization itself is one factor, and the accompanying urbanization—the move from small towns toward cities—disrupted many long-established communities. In some places, even more sinister realities such as colonization or enslavement wrenched families and individuals away from not only their communities but their rich cultural roots as well. Overall, particularly in North America, a spirit of individualism values autonomy above all. Eventually, by the end of World War II, we came to a moment in which "family" was taken first and foremost to mean a nuclear family: parents and their children, living in their own home. Those families were increasingly understood to be units that should manage finances, housing, and childcare without the support of others. By the end of the twentieth century, those families were increasingly isolated, even from one another.

Hard-won experience shows the downsides of this reality. Especially for parents of young children or multiple children, tasks as simple as finding adult companionship each day or getting supper on the table each evening can seem monumental. As children grow older, their immediate, physical needs may lessen a bit, but the need that parents feel for mentors and companions can be even stronger. So what is to be done?

I have already spoken in this chapter of seeing family as church. Here, we might consider the reverse: the benefits that come from seeing church as family, specifically as extended family. This way of thinking lies at the foundation of the Christian tradition itself. Jesus often spoke of his followers as "brothers and sisters," and the earliest Christians took seriously the possibility that they might live concretely as a kind of extended household. For example, one of the earliest roles for deacons was care of the widows within the community. Acts 2 describes the young community in this way: "All who believed were together and had all things in common; they would sell their property and possessions and divide them among all according to each one's need" (vv. 44–45).

Contemporary church members may not be ready to merge their bank accounts, but they can still ask what it might mean to function as an extended household, and particularly with a view to supporting parents. Spelling this out will require careful attention to the specifics of each community, but a few suggestions may spark the conversation.

- Parents can be brought together and given opportunities to form friendships. Adult education or other resources focused especially on parenting is a natural way to do this.

- Important moments for children—baptism or confirmation, for example—are also perfect times to bring together parents for conversation, mutual support, and prayer as it relates to the stage of parenting in which they find themselves.

- Cooperatives of various kinds are a natural outgrowth of these connections. Parents might cooperate in childcare or meal preparation. Other possibilities—older children babysitting younger ones—may emerge.

- The broader church community can step in to support parents in a myriad of ways. I am reminded of a program at one church that felt like a life preserver thrown to my husband and me in the early days of our parenting. On Friday nights, the church organized a significant program of formation and fun activities for children. We parents were strongly encouraged to bring our children and to leave them—so that we could spend time together. During that season, we had almost no time and even less money, but because of that church program, my husband and I got to have a cup of coffee and a conversation at least once a week.

- Adults who are not parents or not actively parenting can lean into relationships, especially with older children and with teenagers, by taking time that parents do not always have to listen and to engage. This always has to be done in a safe way, with appropriate boundaries, but relationships like these can be invaluable.

- Social events where children are welcome and any cost is very low can feel like oxygen to parents whose resources are strained. Our family has benefited from church habits like a weekly Wednesday night supper catered family-style and offered for a modest suggested donation or a church-wide dance where the whole family can come and enjoy an evening together.

- The recent pandemic has taught us the value of in-person interaction, but it has also reminded us that virtual interactions have their place. For single parents, a short meeting for prayer with others in the evening can take place online and serve as a crucial anchor in a busy week.

Again, particularly helpful practicalities will emerge in specific communities. Some parents may need more help with transportation or job-hunting or growing gardens. Some may be hungry for instruction in faith or just for joy-filled celebration. Some families may need laundry facilities or safe after-school spaces. Some may benefit most from a book club meeting in a local coffee shop. Like any family, the extended family of the church has to be attuned to its members, to see what they need most, and to be ready to reach out in love.

4

Toddlers
Not That Terrible

Among parents, toddlers are the stuff of fearful whispers. ("The tantrums!") Toddlerhood, though, is also a phase of discovery, wonder, and intense joy. Watching a toddler who is intent on exploration—whether they are focusing on themselves, on relationships with others, or on the world around them—is one of the most remarkable experiences not only of parenthood but perhaps of the human experience itself.

So where does the apprehension about toddlerhood come from? What is really going on in this phase of life and in this phase of parenting? A lot, as it turns out.

Above all, toddlerhood is a crucial moment for children to "move away" from their parents in new ways—both literally, as they begin to toddle, and in many analogous ways as well. From the parents' point of view, this huge development often leaves them scrambling. Seen from the child's point of view, though, this is a deeply good phase.

Surely one of the most essential elements of our humanity is the possibility of stepping into the world and exercising our will to affect it. For adults, this may have become so familiar that they overlook it. It is essential to the fabric of our being that we *decide to do things and do them*, whether walking to the bus stop, cooking a meal, or planning a party. For the toddler, this is all new. They are beginners in affecting-the-world. Is it any wonder that working it all out takes so much of their energy—and is sometimes frustrating? They have no way to know why it is that walking toward a flower and smelling it earns coos of approval, but walking toward the toy in another child's hand and taking it draws harsh criticism. They can't understand why one afternoon a parent suggests ice cream and—like magic!—they are whisked off to enjoy this sweet treat, but then later that night, when they ask—logically enough!—for more ice cream, the possibility is simply dismissed. And why, after an older sibling is allowed to climb up to the highest point on the playground climbing structure, are they simply told no?

Parents would perhaps do best if they looked at the broad spectrum of a whole set of new skills: (1) identifying goals, (2) planning execution, (3) taking action, and (4) negotiating with others. As is the case when they learn to ride a bike, what children need most are adults who are trotting alongside, offering encouragement, putting out a steadying hand, and scooping them up when a fall does happen. The noes inevitably must be given, but they can be delivered with kindness and solidarity. Parents continue in their own analogous processes of learning what they can change and what they can't, while dealing with the attendant frustration. Parents can see new demonstrations of will not primarily as a problem but as the growth of a crucial ability. As with riding a bike, a lot can go wrong, but the emerging skill is a thrilling one.

Christian parents can even recognize deep theological connections. The Christian tradition is clear: human beings are not created simply for compliance. They are created to learn this intricate dance of knowing and directing their own will toward the good. God does not compel, nor does he simply shape behaviors through punishment and reward. The glory of God is seen in the human person, says Irenaeus, who is "fully alive." God has created these little people to explore, to love, to puzzle, to try even when they fail. It is as they direct their whole selves toward the good, and toward God, that they become who they were meant to be. Perhaps nothing is more important in the energetic, exhausting years of toddlerhood than to rejoice in these little humans who are learning by trial and error what "fully alive" looks and feels like.

What about discipline? Isn't this also part of these years? Indeed, it is. Among the things that toddlers must learn about the world is that it has other people in it, other people who have their own desires and agendas, and that it has limits. Their spirited new expressions of will inevitably meet many obstacles. It is important to remember the long-term goal here, though: to introduce children to these limits with love and to build in them skills of patience and restraint, while also nurturing the beauty and dignity of their God-given wills. This is, after all, a lifelong process.

Closely related to this development of will is self-awareness and self-regulation. Not only is their engagement with the world blooming, but toddlers themselves are changing fast, and this makes for a day-to-day experience that produces marked highs and lows of joy, curiosity, frustration, fear, and, finally, exhaustion. Any given day can be a roller coaster, with the toddler engaged in at least two big tasks: to learn what these experiences are and what they feel like, and to learn how to respond to them. To do that, one thing is needed: a caretaker and companion who—sometimes right by their side, sometimes a few steps back—is ready to describe the path and to lead them forward. Sometimes this is done in direct relation to the toddler herself: "You seem like you're feeling a little sad right now. Can I give you a hug? We all feel sad sometimes, don't we?" Toddlers learn not only through explicit interaction with the caregiver but also through observation. The adult caregiver who is aware of her own ups and downs, and who responds to them with self-compassion, with forbearance, and with determination, is perhaps the most valuable resource a toddler can have. In the space opened up by interaction with such an adult, a toddler can learn ways to not simply suppress emotion but weave it into a life wherein frustration and joy become part of a whole—a whole that is ordered toward purpose, joy, and love.

This may also be the moment children begin to be cared for by adults other than family members. Toddlers are able to interact with siblings in new ways. Preschool, daycare, and playdates may offer new kinds of connections with peers. All these relationships create the foundation of a new world of social connections. Toddlers are only just starting out here. We should not expect that they know the rules of social engagement or that they will possess highly developed empathy. They are, however, learning central lessons. Engagement with others can be fascinating and confusing and frustrating and deeply rewarding. And they are, whether this is intended or not, developing a normative template for relationships. If those around them are responsive, they learn to expect that others will see and respond to them. If those around them are distant and distracted, they learn to expect that. People—especially parents who are reliable, warm, and positive—are all "teaching" in a long-lasting way what relationship is supposed to look like. Toddlerhood is an essential moment when children can learn that they are seen, known, and loved, and that they are being incorporated into a larger social web where they can expect a fundamental level of reliability and safety. Somewhat paradoxically, this kind of beginning sets the stage for adults who are most ready to live fully and to take risks where needed. It is also essential to the development of discipline mentioned earlier. In a world where they can trust their caregivers, toddlers are ultimately able to accept the noes that sometimes make no sense to them at all. It is in a world where there is reasonable promise of good things to come that self-restraint makes sense.

Among all the experiences of toddlerhood, we might also dwell a bit longer on the unique capacity in toddlerhood for wonder and joy. This is the time for running through grass and dipping toes into the water, tasting new foods and reaching out to pet an animal, drawing first pictures and telling stories and giving hugs. This ability to see the thing as it is, in all its specificity, and delight in it, is sometimes dulled later in life, but it is essential to our lives as human beings and people of faith. It is well worth celebrating and fostering in our toddlers. Especially for parents of faith, this capacity—which is sometimes overlooked or sentimentalized—can be seen for what it is: the beginning of life in a world that is created for beauty and good.

Every one of these remarkable elements of toddlerhood is integral to setting the stage for faith. A person who desires things, and sets a course to gain them; a person who knows what it is to be in relationship, and especially to be in relationship with one who can be trusted; a person who lives in a web of community; a person who knows how to delight—this is a person who can move into a living faith. To live these things out every day is certainly most important. As toddlers acquire language, parents can speak explicitly about them, when appropriate. In a Christian tradition, where there is a crucial place for proclamation by word, toddlerhood offers the first moments for parents to speak about their faith with their children and, even more, to invite their children into this experience. Even in these early years, parents can speak about fundamental matters.

- They can speak of God as Creator of all things.
- They can speak of God as a friend who is always close, though unseen.
- They can speak of forgiveness—and model it.
- They can begin to tell the stories of the Christian tradition, especially those involving children—from Moses in his little ark of safety, to David's unexpected victory over a strong foe, to Jesus's welcome of children.
- Especially, they can begin to know Jesus as teacher, as friend, and as one who exercises authority in the ways described above.

And, of course, toddlers can be invited into living the life of the church, along with their caregivers:

- Participating in worship and singing along
- Beginning to memorize simple prayers and songs
- Extending care and compassion, even in small ways
- Participating in habits such as blessings at meals and folding hands in prayer or making the sign of the cross

As we consider all the rich elements of this toddler stage, we should note that parents of toddlers may well be having their own experiences as well. These are often the most physically demanding years of parenting. Suddenly, caretaking involves running after a newly mobile child, looking out for new dangers, and negotiating with a child who has a will of her own. Toddlerhood for one child often corresponds with other experiences too: a parent may return to work, a new baby may join the family, or parents may simply be working through the awareness—with the end of this first "baby stage"—of how quickly each of these stages will pass.

It can also bring connection with other parents as toddlers take part in daycare, preschool, or play groups. "The parents of my children's peers," or even just "fellow parents," becomes a category for some for the first time. This camaraderie can bring its own joys and challenges: a sense of community, perhaps, as parents watch their children learn and grow together, but at the same time, the first inklings of comparison or even competition can appear. This is the time to support parents and remind them that each child, and each family, has their own way forward. Differences in gifts and weaknesses, in rates of maturation and in the challenges that appear along the way, are not only possible but inevitable. This is the time for the church to model—and to include parents in—community that is marked by support and solidarity. This is especially important given the fact, as noted in chapter 3, that parents often must make their way without the support of a community and extended family that was more likely in the past.

As parents are able to glimpse the richness of the toddler phase, and as they are supported in the demands that toddlerhood brings, they can experience great joy. What is more exciting than a child's first steps? And there are so many different kinds of "first steps" here. Ideally, toddlerhood, even with its challenges, is a time for celebration, as both family and community cheer this little one on.

5

Mapmaking and Apprenticeship

In a book on parenting, we should probably ask the question: "What *is* parenting, exactly?" I don't mean that we should ask about the *goal* of parenting, although that is certainly connected. And most parents do have some sense that their parenting efforts are directed to certain ends. They want to move children toward being functioning adults, or perhaps good citizens. Parents of faith may have an explicit goal of handing on that faith and fostering in their children a meaningful relationship with God or with the church. If they are thinking more specifically, parents may have other goals: to raise children to be happy, to be thoughtful, to be kind; to value education or family; and to live fruitful lives. Goals of these sorts matter, but they make sense only insofar as parents take the fundamental step of asking what the fundamental reality of parenting involves.

Three common models of parenting come immediately to mind: provision, instruction, and discipline. All parents know that providing and caring for children is essential to their task. From the first baby blanket to a college education, parents must ask what their children need (and sometimes what they want), and then determine whether and how they can meet those needs. The model of instruction is central for most parents. Parents teach everything from how to hold a fork, to the habit of saying "thank you," to ways to understand people and the larger world. Finally, even if it is not what they most look forward to, the majority of parents would name "discipline" as a central model for what they are doing as parents—and for some, this would top the list.

I would not suggest that we simply erase any of those ways of imagining what parenting involves, but I do want to offer other models that I believe to be richer ones. They serve to expand our imagination about this work, and—perhaps unexpectedly—they also yield many practical kinds of encouragement and direction for parents.

The first model is that of mapmaking. To see the model fully, imagine a parent seated at a desk, a large sheet of paper in front of them, and a child (or children) seated on their lap. The process of parenting, I am suggesting, is something like sketching out a map as the child watches. Explicitly—and even more powerfully, implicitly—a parent "tells" a child what the world is like. This includes, of course, forms of instruction. ("If you want to get to here, you'll have to walk this way.") It is a more multilayered and profound kind of instruction than a straightforward explanation of how to travel from A to B.

Mapmaking involves sketching out possibilities and edges. It means marking dangers. ("Here is a tall mountain range. And over there? Dragons.") It means deciding which features and details are included. (The height of mountain ranges? The best spot to stop and see the view?) It will, of course, reflect the parent's own knowledge and experience in many ways. Roads that she has traveled herself will be detailed and precise, and others may be indicated only vaguely. Or there may be places parents have never been, but where they very much want their children to go, and those will be drawn with vivid colors. The map may also be inaccurate—and parents do their children a favor if they remember that. For better or worse, a map does two things: it notes certain locations, and it has a center and an orientation around which these locations are placed. Parents cannot simply throw up their hands and say, "I have no idea."

In particular, parents place an X on the map that marks a crucial spot for their children: "You are here." Parents don't simply sketch a world; they also tell children that they are part of this world, with varying relationships to various places. They indicate that some things are near and some things are far, as well as how the child might get from here to there.

For parents of faith, imagining a map also offers possibilities beyond simply speaking of a divine person called "God" or a reality called "church." It means thinking about the center of the map and its fundamental orientation. To sketch faith for a child means drawing a map in which true north is a God who is good, a God who is love. It means suggesting both a spot on the map and also invaluable travel companions that together make "the church." The "you" indicated on the map, moreover, has not been shipwrecked in that spot accidentally but is placed and is beloved, connected to God and to a company of saints. This map will also include an awareness of sin: signs pointing out spots that are dangerous, or the traveler's own tendency to become disoriented. Faith may move parents to mark other spots in specific ways, but it is the central orientation that is most important, and on which all else must be built.

Of course, this gives parents very interesting questions to ask of themselves: What is the map that I am drawing? What is the map that I have drawn so far? These are not easy questions to answer. So much of this is known deeply and intuitively, and parents may well not realize what they are communicating. Here, a secondary practice of mapmaking could come in handy: narration of, and conversation about, the contours of this particular map. In the model of mapmaking I am offering, a parent might speak as she sketches. ("Here is a small stream. It's bigger in summer and smaller and winter, although that's hard to see here. Here is a great city. Your grandfather and I visited there once.") And, just as important, a parent asks questions. ("Over here is a desert. Do you know what plants you would find there?") As a child grows, those questions will change, and a parent will not simply describe but will hear their child's impressions too. ("Have you gone this way? What did you find?")

Over time, a new phenomenon appears: each child is building her own map (the map that she will pass on to her own children, perhaps). A child's map will always differ somewhat from the parent's, and it may differ greatly. In later chapters, I discuss the dynamics of parenting teenagers and adults, but suffice to say here that parents are called both to offer their own map and to cheer on the child who begins to imagine her own. Even if adult children decide that this map they have been given is all wrong, they have at least seen a map made. They know to look for pathways and water sources. They know that maps are for sharing and using with others.

This model of mapmaking, it must be admitted, relies more on categories of picturing and discussing than on doing. For the latter category, I want to suggest another model of parenting, one that I understand to be even more comprehensive and important: we can think of parent and child as involved in a process of apprenticeship.

Apprenticeship, which still survives in some of the arts and some of the trades, was once a dominant form of education. The basic form is a simple one: an apprentice works alongside a master, watching carefully and slowly moving into greater and greater participation in the work. A masonry apprentice learns bricklaying by watching and then joining in the work of a master bricklayer. In the art studio, an apprentice might be allowed first to clean brushes, then to mix paint, then to begin adding details to paintings. Apprentices to the great artists of the Renaissance did these very things. Leonardo DaVinci, for example, became an apprentice at fourteen as part of a chain of apprenticeship that was eventually a chain of masters. He studied under a master named Andrea del Rocco, who himself had studied under Donatello. The apprentice eventually receives payment and produces her own masterpieces. The master, close at hand, oversees this process throughout.

Too often, parenting (and, in a sense, even the term "parenting" itself) slides toward imagining something that parents are doing *to* their children. Parents can get pulled into something perhaps better described as management of children. We get them ready for the day. We feed them; we bathe them; we pick them up and bandage wounds. And we try to follow all the advice. When they are newborns, we try to put them to sleep on their backs. When they attend school, we try to set up space for them to do their homework. We try to praise them more often than we criticize them. Ultimately, though—and sometimes it seems almost ceaselessly—parents are doing things to and for our children. This model has real weaknesses. It can create anxiety in children. It can erode the relationship between parent and child. And all this management, frankly, is exhausting—both for parents and for children. The model of apprenticeship, on the other hand, offers a number of fruitful emphases for parents.

The model of apprenticeship is more about parents simply being with their children, doing life together. If it becomes a guiding model, then it actually leads to less vigilance and less alarm. It involves less planning and less organizing. It involves more presence, more patience, more playfulness, and more calm. The calling of a mother or a father to walk with their children, sharing work, sharing play, sharing *themselves*, is a richer reality.

If I were to draw on lived experience, I would say that this picture of parenting actually looks something more like what we tend to associate with extended family members spending time with children. Picture an aunt or uncle who's involved, who knows a child well, and who spends time with the child regularly. A certain overarching dimension of simple companionship is evident. Grandparents, famously, are always more relaxed.

Parents are likely to immediately respond, "Of course grandparents are more relaxed! They don't have the same responsibility for the outcome!" This kind of relaxed vision may seem unrealistic. In my own parenting, I have found that it is more effective, and more practical, than we might imagine. It can include teaching, but it does not rest on constant, explicit instruction.

And interestingly enough, the focus of the master is not even on the apprentice in a direct way. Of course, the master will keep one eye toward the apprentice to see what it is that she does well, or even to offer a word of correction. There is a fundamental way, however, in which the two are faced together toward the thing that they are doing—together. It may be a subtle difference, but there is something important in this model: the child is not a product but a beloved person.

To fill out the picture of apprenticeship, there are at least two other essential elements of the model that I have in mind. First, I think of the way that many parents concern themselves with "getting it right" at every stage of their parenting journey. There is nothing wrong with a desire to do well, but in an age of social media and comparison, this can become suffocating. To talk of the work of apprenticing one's children need not mean that one's own mastery of everything is complete. In the apprenticeship of parenting, part of what a parent shares is her own ongoing learning process. Practically speaking, a child who sees her parent apologize, and even more, a child who sees her parent apologize *to her*, is being apprenticed in an important way.

Second, children are not apprenticed *only* to their parents. Children learn in a studio filled with artists; they learn *in community*. This is perhaps the single most important point in a book dedicated to supporting faith-filled parenting. Parents can seek out communities who will contribute to their children's apprenticeship, but they cannot conjure them from nothing. Ideally, parents are welcomed, along with their children, into communities that are already functioning in this way.

There may be programs or various forms of religious instruction in communities that can function as a form of apprenticeship, especially when we remember that the goal here is not simply conveying information. Initiatives like clubs and camps and classes are most valuable when they set the stage for the real work of apprenticeship: the long, patient process by which more experienced people come alongside those less experienced and share with them the most valuable resource of all, which is themselves. They offer a context to do the work of the body of Christ—worshiping, serving, building, celebrating, and mourning—together.

It's important to keep in mind a crucial challenge to apprenticeship parenting. In our post-industrialized world, we are often at odds with this model. In other settings, past and present, parents and children were and are literally able to work together because the work of the parents was not by definition separate from something that children were able to do. Probably the simplest and most obvious example here is a family farm. In that world, children as young as five are needed to work together with their parents. We are in a different situation. What we call "work," by which we usually mean paid work, now usually means traveling away from home and being gone, sometimes for ten or twelve hours at a time. It is true that some parents are able to do the work at home, and that can provide some relief. But it can also highlight even more sharply the fact that adult work usually does not mix well with the care of children.

I don't want to simply romanticize the past. Living in the wake of some of these changes, though, parents can keep this challenge in mind. Parents can seek out stretches of time with their children in which they are not pursuing activities or entertainment, but are working together purposefully for some end. I have known parents, for example, who resisted buying or repairing a dishwasher for just this reason. The time spent washing and drying dishes is a perfect example of the sort of time in which the work of apprenticeship is given space to happen.

Christian parents may notice that this model of apprenticeship is a familiar one. Apprenticeship could be a way of thinking of discipleship. In Jesus, God became present for a process of apprenticeship, first with the Twelve, and then with ever-expanding circles of Christians. As Christian parents seek to imitate God, they can see their own commitment to the intensive process of apprenticeship parenting as a reflection of Jesus's own work among those he loved.

An important question remains to be asked: If parents are like masters, and children are like apprentices, then what is the skill that these apprentices are learning? It's not painting or stonework, of course. What is it that parents are modeling?

We could answer the question in a couple of different ways. On the one hand, children are apprenticed to parents to learn a million things: how to talk, how to tie a shoe, how to drive a car. On the other hand, underneath all of those things, there are much more profound things being modeled and learned. Even in the case of experienced parents, there can be profound value in stepping back and reflecting on this question: What are the things at the center? What is it that we are teaching our children most fundamentally? Such an important question might even deserve very focused and intentional consideration in the form of a retreat or weekly time of reflection. For couples parenting together, it could be the basis of a rich, ongoing conversation.

As a way to begin that conversation, I want to suggest three possible answers that one might give about the fundamental character of parenting. These are hoped-for skills that have anchored parenting for me (even when I have fallen short in giving them the priority I intend!).

First is the most important of all—even if it is not the first topic addressed in typical parenting books: we are teaching our children

joy. By "joy," I don't particularly mean cheerfulness. I don't necessarily mean a "good mood," and I certainly do not mean putting
on blinders to avoid painful realities and negative emotions. What
I mean is a deep conviction underlying all else—that the world is
good and beautiful, and that one is welcomed into it. This includes
a sense of wonder at this deeply good reality, and it inevitably results
in gratitude, both for the smallest details and also for the remarkable
gift that existence itself is.

Second is a sense of purpose. Here I mean seeing myself *in the
world* as an agent, as someone who is interacting in it and with it in
meaningful ways. We have already noted how helpful it can be to see
this as a fundamental good being accomplished in toddlers, as they
try to find ways to change their own situation—and the world around
them. The same could be said for teenagers. It is easy to become
focused on only setting limits, but parents can also look for ways to
celebrate their children's growing abilities with them.

Third, in this world of beauty—a world in which children are
also able to accomplish things and bring about change—parents are
apprenticing children to a sense of deep connection to others, and
to the obligation to respond to others with compassion. Parents give
children a great gift when they embody the art of living in a web of
community and connection.

Of course, for parents of faith there is a sense in which the practice of that faith sits at the very center of it all. Ultimately, though,
conscious faith rests on and incorporates all of these. Wonder at the
beauty of the world proceeds as an awareness of God's *personal* presence and produces trust, gratitude, and a deep sense of being beloved.
A sense of purpose becomes a vocation, a calling to live one's own
individual life to God's glory. And a broad sense of connection to
others finds a crucial center in connection to, and commitment to,
the church—a connection that constantly spills over in the habit of
loving others and inviting others to the table.

Here is the heart of parenting: to live life immersed in joy, purpose,
compassion, and faith—and to share that life with children.

This model of apprenticeship presents a profound challenge to parents: they must ask in what sense they are a "master" of these skills.
Several decades ago a parenting book was published that emphasized

how profoundly children can be influenced. The title of the book: *Children Are Wet Cement*. Some years later I heard another parenting expert refer to this book, saying that the title of the book is right, but perhaps not in the way parents expect. Children *are* deeply shaped by parents, but parents should not so much imagine that they are intentionally sculpting children into what they want them to be. Rather, children are wet cement whose parents fall face-first into them. Parents do leave an imprint, but it is an imprint of who they themselves are. This influence, this presence, is far more important than any strategies or tricks they could take up.

The Growing Years

As children move from toddlerhood into their growing-up years, a new world opens up for them and for their parents. These are the years where conscious memories begin to form, and where the "story" of each family really takes root and grows. In the children themselves, a foundation is laid for the people they will be for the rest of their lives. It is a rich and consequential time.

In children, remarkable intellectual and emotional growth take place. Children begin to make friends, to understand and analyze the world around them, and to navigate that world—more and more on their own. The outline of each individual child's tendencies appears even more clearly than it has earlier, including each child's interests, gifts, challenges, and all the little things that make them themselves. A child at ten years old is so different from a toddler in every way.

It is perhaps worth it to pause here, to turn attention back to those newborn days. In the hazy early days of infancy, parents are often transfixed by their children (despite their sleep deprivation!). As children grow and become independent, parents continue to have the task and the privilege of communicating to their children that they *delight* in them. Even before parents show their appreciation for individual accomplishments, before they congratulate their children on jobs well done, before they express their pride, their calling as parents is to take joy in the child herself. As with so many of the tasks of parenting, this is a message communicated not in word but in action. Children simply know when a parent takes joy in them, takes joy simply in being in their presence. At every stage of parenting, after all, Christian parents seek to parent as God does, and there is no element of God's posture toward us more elemental than this joy or delight. That foundation will be crucial in these years where occasional correction or specific expression of disapproval must take place.

Jesus himself offers an example. The story is often retold, so we may need to take a moment to see it with fresh eyes. At one point in Jesus's teaching ministry, those who are coming to see and hear him bring small children to ask for a blessing. Jesus's disciples are concerned about this interruption and try to stop them. Jesus corrects them, saying, "Let the children come to me, and do not prevent them; for the kingdom of heaven belongs to such as these" (Matt. 19:14). It's a beautiful saying, with many implications. For our purposes, though, the most striking thing is the simple center of this incident. Though he is in the midst of important work, Jesus responds to these children with an open heart. He is ready to be present to them, and his correction to his disciples suggests that his first response to these children does not have to do with managing them or changing them in some way, but rather simply with recognizing a particular gift connected to their age: they remind their elders of what it means to be able to receive the kingdom of God. There is nothing sentimentalized or idealized about this. Jesus offers us an example of the fundamental stance that should characterize our relationship with small children: a readiness to say, "Come to me," and to appreciate the gifts they bring.

In this openness and in the connection it creates, these growing years become the most important years for the kind of apprenticeship mentioned in chapter 5. At six or eight or ten years old, children are profoundly ready to enter into both relationship and practice, and to follow along in a great many family activities. These are years to fill with family habits and stories and conversations. Especially if the first years of parenting necessarily involved some disruption and disorganization, these years are the perfect time to dig in and to look for ways to establish fruitful patterns.

One such practice deserves special consideration: the family table. A habit of gathering and eating together is crucial, especially for families who will spend some or most of the day apart. For our family, even

when it was hard to put a meal together, and even when it was hard
to get us all together at the same time, this habit has been an anchor
that has kept us connected. For families where work schedules or
other obstacles intervene, a shared meal can happen less frequently or
at a time other than the evening. Eaten together regularly, a Saturday
morning brunch can bring many of the same benefits.

This tradition will work best if it is not left only to one person—
often Mom—and can become an exercise in cooperation. Even young
children can bring napkins to the table or get a vote regarding the
menu. ("Should we have spaghetti or stew tomorrow?") Older kids
can set and clear the table, rinse dishes, and so on. Ideally, even cooking the meal is a responsibility that can rotate to some extent. In this
way, children become not only the ones benefiting from this habit but
the ones enacting it.

For families of faith, this habit of sharing the table is especially
important, as these meals can become a crucial point of sharing faith.
A blessing said before dinner is perhaps the simplest example, but
there are many other examples. Some families give children an opportunity to voice prayer requests before the main blessing is prayed,
thus bringing their own concerns to this small, shared liturgy. As these
meals stretch across the span of a year, they can be a time for other
celebrations. Family birthdays or anniversaries can be a time to say
a prayer especially suited for the occasion at hand.

And ecclesial celebrations can find a place too. In Advent our
family often sings just the chorus of "Oh, Come Let Us Adore Him"
as our table blessing. In Lent we sometimes read a short passage of
Scripture at the table. On saints' feast days we might cook a meal that
is especially appropriate, and we are much more likely to have dessert in celebration. Especially when faith can sometimes be reduced
to "being good," meals like these remind us that joy stands at the
center of the Christian life.

Hospitality also sits at the heart of the Christian tradition, whether
it is the "hospitality" that God shows to human beings or the hospitality we are called to extend to one another. How do our children
come to know this as a lived reality? For our family, a regular habit of
eating together has allowed us to extend our table and offer hospitality to others. We have had the opportunity to welcome friends and

neighbors, and (especially when holidays leave people with nowhere to go) sometimes strangers. One of the most remarkable rewards of becoming the parent of young adults is that my husband and I have begun to be invited to their tables as well.

Of course, the table is not the only place for regular family prayer. For many families, the morning includes a car trip to school, and that can be an ideal moment for a short prayer of blessing for the day. Bedtime serves as an ideal moment for prayer, giving a chance to recollect the day and to offer it to God. Just before bed, Catholic families might gather as a whole to pray the Rosary—or at least a decade of the Rosary—together. Some parents invite their children to a simplified version of a nightly Examen.

The daily Examen (or an Examen of Consciousness) is a prayerful method of asking how God has been present in our day, how we have responded to that presence, and how we might grow in holiness. With young children, it could be as simple as (1) settling into a prayerful attitude, (2) reviewing the most memorable events of the day, (3) asking how God was present and how the child responded, and (4) inviting the child to pray in response: "What do we want to tell Jesus about what happened today?" (Parents can model simple words of praise, thankfulness, repentance, and forgiveness, as well as prayers for the grace to draw close to God in the coming day.)

Bedtime is also the perfect time for reading together. Reading the Bible is always a possibility, and there is also a growing number of beautiful children's books related to faith. Reading books of every kind can serve the fundamental purposes of settling down to sleep, of connecting parent and child, and of building a repertoire of stories they have in common. Sharing lists of books that are especially worth reading, and perhaps even sharing the books themselves, would be one way that communities and Christian parents and churches could support families in this life-giving habit.

Traveling together can also allow for forms of apprenticing in family life. Inhabiting a new space and seeing new sights expands the imagination of all, but the act of stepping away from typical obligations and distractions often allows for deeper and more focused interaction. Family vacations to spots of historical value or great natural beauty are a well-known tradition, but when we see them in the context of apprenticeship, our perspective shifts a bit. The goal need not be an exotic or impressive destination—a consoling thought especially for families whose budgets are tight! Even a day trip can give the opportunity to see something new and to have a meal and a conversation that matters along the way. Among the activities that can be part of a family vacation, our family has found that worshiping in an unfamiliar church can offer an unexpected benefit: a reminder that the church is bigger than just our own local community.

Other possibilities for family traditions during children's growing years are wide and varied, limited only by creativity and the particulars of each family's life. Families can celebrate the rhythm of life in regular ways by

- enjoying Saturday morning pancakes;
- celebrating weekly traditions like game night, movie night, or pizza night;
- singing or listening to certain music in the car or at the dinner table;
- organizing backyard "campouts" in warmer weather; or
- going for a walk or hike in the same place or at the same time regularly.

Families can connect to others by

- sharing childcare with a few trusted friends;
- setting up a "supper club" with a small number of other families, visiting one another's homes on a rotating basis rather than eating out; or
- creating particular rituals with a small number of other families—perhaps celebrating the last day of school with ice cream together.

Families can serve others by

- bringing a meal or baked goods to neighbors who are lonely or in crisis;

- serving together at soup kitchens or other ministries of outreach to the poor;
- serving the poor through activities at home—making sandwiches or "care kits," for example, to be given to those who are unhoused;
- raising money together to give away; or
- inviting others into their home who need housing or companionship (where circumstances allow).

The list could go on. Each family will have to find its own pattern of traditions, tied to its own character as a family and its own limits. No family can do all these things, and so a sense of the particular habits that fit each family best is essential. This in turn will mean saying no to proposals that are inherently good ones but are simply too much for a particular family to add to their load. This is truly a situation where "less is more." As chapter 8 will describe, social media has exacerbated a temptation to imagine these family moments as a kind of commodity to be orchestrated and displayed. As chapter 11 will discuss, families have to resist trying to do everything and especially trying to compare themselves to others. The habit of simply delighting in children and the model of apprenticeship suggest something else. Above all, these are moments to be together, to share life together. Parents will have to discern which habits they will build and where these traditions can be incorporated. Often the most practical reality involves traditions that are simple and organically connected to the rest of life.

The shared life of the family, as some of these examples already suggest, should ideally include elements of work and service, as well as play and celebration. In chapter 3 we considered ways in which work has been separated from family for many in this post-industrial world. For families who do not live on a family farm or work in a family-owned business, the need arises to imagine when and where they can work together—and how they should do that.

For most such families, there is already a category of "chores" at play. Just a couple suggestions may serve to expand and strengthen that category. First, especially in these younger years, parents can look for opportunities to assign chores in a shared way. A parent paired with a child, or two siblings paired together, can take on a task together. Or a time can be set aside—perhaps Saturday morning—when everyone is working on chores at the same time. Working together gives parents an opportunity to create a certain "culture of work": an attitude that sees the work as fundamentally good, even in the smallest detail, so that it is not simply something to hurry through but something to attend to, with purpose. The Christian tradition is clear that the work of human hands and minds exists *not* as a necessary evil but rather as a good. It is a way that human beings can imitate God's own creativity. In some of his recent writings, Pope Francis has offered another striking observation: it is in the family that people learn care for a "common home."[1] Coming together to care for a family home teaches children that the world they enter as adults requires the same kind of attention in many ways, including environmental care.

The model of apprenticeship takes on new dimensions when we remember that there are mentors other than parents. Chapter 3 mentioned the ways in which nuclear families now tend to be isolated from extended families and from a larger community. One of the great losses resulting from this isolation is that children have less opportunity for meaningful, ongoing forms of apprenticeship to adults other than their parents. There is hope though.

First, families might be reminded and encouraged in building bonds with extended family. During our own children's growing-up years, we spent significant time and effort to get to an annual Cousin Camp at the home of our children's grandparents. The children spent many hours together in these long summer days, but they also spent time with other adults in their family. They went hunting with their uncle; they went to a horse auction with their grandfather. They spent time in the kitchen with their grandmother, talking and laughing. Now that our children are older, it is easy to see how a certain foundation was built in those years. Our children saw other models of adulthood—models of work and marriage—up close. They saw their parents in the context of other long-term adult relationships. It was a long drive to those Cousin Camps, but it was worth it.

Grandparents, in particular, can be an invaluable resource in this ongoing task of apprenticeship, bringing both insights gleaned from years of their own parenting and also the long-term perspective that comes only from having moved through and beyond those years. Many families already look for ways to connect to grandparents, but the apprenticeship model may suggest a way to shape these interactions. A trip to Disney World may create excitement that children will always remember, but it does not easily offer opportunities for apprenticeship to the realities of daily life. Time spent with grandparents can also be quieter time, eating together, reading and singing and dancing together, and taking up small tasks together in a way that connects work with the pleasure of a particularly rich companionship.

Other adults in the community can also provide mentorship to children. Teachers and coaches can both offer models that shape children's most fundamental ways of thinking about the world. As we recognize the potential impact of these relationships, a related possibility comes into focus. The church can and should be a place where children find other adults with whom they can share life.

When we think about other mentors in the community, a painful topic must be raised. We cannot consider the possibility of our children connecting with other adults unless we address the danger that some adults may pose. Unfortunately, parents must pay close attention to other adults who single children out as "special," who give them unexpected gifts, or who initiate periods of time alone. There is never any reason for another adult to engage in private communication with a child online, or by text or phone. Parents can also be proactive by speaking to children from a young age about what inappropriate touching looks like, by reminding them that adults should never need them to keep secrets from their parents, and by generally reassuring children regularly that they are ready and available to talk, if anything ever "feels funny" to the child. In many cases, parents simply have a vague sense that something is off, and it is always the best thing if they take their intuitions seriously.

Churches must rigorously vet those who will come into contact with children, and when they look for red flags. Churches should take the time to initiate the conversations that make it hard for those with dark intentions to isolate and prey on individual children. All of this is difficult to talk about and difficult even to think about.

Approaching the matter directly, however, actually serves to open up the possibilities for children to find connections with other adults that can be deeply life-giving.

I can picture the very moment, fifty years ago, when I was a kindergartener taking part in our children's program at church. It was a moment when the children were engaged in a variety of activities, moving through different parts of the room. I was sitting quietly with a book. Our teacher, Mrs. Cherry, spoke with a kind voice when she stopped to talk with me for a moment and eventually asked me if I would like to "invite Jesus into my heart." I did. All the years since then—my whole life of faith and life in the church and the study and teaching of theology—have a crucial beginning in that moment, when Mrs. Cherry took my hand and showed me the way forward.

These elementary years also bring new challenges and busyness as families navigate commitments and demands. Parents who are married have to negotiate again how they will inhabit new patterns of family life without being pulled apart. In households with multiple children, relationships between siblings must be worked out. And, as parents already know well, new technologies have created unprecedented challenges in the way they demand attention from parents and children alike. Each of these issues is significant enough that it is treated elsewhere in this book. For the moment, focusing on the many possibilities of this stage enables us to direct our energy to the positive.

Taken together, these elements describe the way that as children grow, and as parents grow further into their role as parents, a family comes into its own. Each family will have its own particular strengths and vulnerabilities, and its own unfolding story that makes it what it is. This individuality is something to be treasured, much as we would do with an individual person. Just as individuals are transformed by Christ in particular ways, so too we can imagine Christian families of many different kinds. There is not just one way to be a family of faith!

At the same time, there are ideals we can hold up for all families. In these years, family becomes the place that children come more fully to know what it means to be welcomed and loved. In these years, they have a chance to be incorporated into communities and purposes that are bigger than themselves, to direct their energies purposefully, and to experience what it means to work consistently toward particular ends. Essential building blocks, like joy and a sense of their own dignity and purpose, can be laid for the rest of their lives.

We spoke of Jesus's encounter with children above, but we could also note the single Gospel account from the book of Luke that gives a window into Jesus's own childhood. When he is twelve, Jesus accompanies Mary and Joseph and a large group of extended family to Jerusalem to observe Passover. At the conclusion of the festival, they all begin to travel home. Only after they have been on the road for a full day do Mary and Joseph realize that Jesus is nowhere among his relatives. They rush back to Jerusalem, and it takes a full three days for them to find him in the temple courts among the teachers there. When they express their great worry, he answers only by saying, "Did you not know that I must be in my Father's house?" (2:49).

None of our children are God incarnate, but the story tells us a great deal. Every part of human existence is consecrated by God's entry into it. Just as we can say generally "God became human," we can say more specifically "God became a child." In this passage, we see not only Jesus's own character but also a picture of childhood that reminds us of its dignity and beauty. Worried parents will always search for their children, but Jesus's answer reminds us that they often have their own calling, and they are pursuing it. In this, it is our privilege to accompany them.

The Art of Discipline

Books telling parents how to discipline children are everywhere. Count to three. Use logic. Talk so they will listen. That is not the aim of this chapter. My hope here is to reflect a bit on discipline in a larger context, and to ask how others can support parents in this task.

What is "discipline" anyway? In general, we use the term simply to mean encouraging some behaviors and discouraging others. And this, without question, is part of a parent's task. Teaching a child to say please or to take turns gives her valuable habits of respect for others. Learning not to throw things at people will make her experiences in the world go much better. The model of parenting as apprenticeship, however, suggests something more. For our purposes in this chapter I would suggest that discipline can be more fruitfully imagined as apprenticing children to gather their energies together and to direct them to the purposes of love.

This larger definition helps us keep in mind several realities. First, discipline happens in the context of a relationship, one that involves important connection, modeling, and guiding, and not simply correction. Children's challenging behaviors must be seen in that context. Second, the task of discipline primarily involves not parents shaping their children but children gaining the skills that will allow them to act purposefully in the world. And perhaps most importantly, this definition of discipline suggests that what parents should aim to teach children above all is not to be respectable or simply to be compliant but to *love*.

"Love" may sound like a lofty goal here, but isn't love what ought to guide us in everything? "Which is the first of all the commandments?" one of the scribes asks Jesus in Mark 12:28. And this is a reasonable question. We all have many obligations and responsibilities. What is it that governs them all? Jesus replies, "The first is this: 'Hear, O Israel! The Lord our God is Lord alone! You shall love the Lord your God with all your heart, with all your soul, with all your mind, and with all your strength.' The second is this: 'You shall love your neighbor as yourself'" (vv. 29–31). Love of God and love of neighbor (and love of oneself, since Jesus assumes that as well) offer a way to understand all the many, smaller tasks that we take up as directed to a larger purpose. If we want a three-year-old to learn not to hit a sibling out of frustration, this should not be simply because we want her to "be nice" but because we want her to learn to love others. If we teach a child to be truthful, we do so because it is a way to love others—and, we could also say, to love God and love oneself. Parents will not always speak explicitly of these larger purposes, but in all cases it will be fruitful to keep them in mind. They may even help determine what parents ask of children and when.

To love in this threefold way—to love God, neighbor, and self—is a big task, and gathering one's energies together actually requires quite a number of skills, including at least the following:

1. To know what one wants to do
2. To know what is possible
3. To persist in the face of obstacles
4. To respond to requests from others
5. To exercise the trust in parents (and sometimes others) required to accede to requests and directions, even when they conflict with one's own impulses
6. To delay gratification and forego a lesser, immediate good for a greater, future one
7. Even in the face of frustration or disappointment, to maintain the emotional regulation that allows for all of the above

8. Eventually, to move into empathy: to see what the world looks like from another's point of view

9. Ultimately, to move into adult levels of self-discipline

Considering these tasks together makes it easier to see several things. First, the tasks that must be learned are numerous, and they are interrelated in complicated ways. Simply beginning by recognizing the complexity of all that a child must accomplish can help put the parental work of "discipline" in perspective. Reading through such a list also reminds us that every one of us continues to develop these skills, and that every one of us sometimes fails. Parental interactions with children can thus be fundamentally rooted in empathy and solidarity. Second, thinking in terms of acquisition of skills helps remind parents to keep a child's physical, emotional, cognitive, and spiritual development at the forefront of their minds. Like any skill, these skills are learned gradually, and children who are just beginners will do best when approached with gentleness and patience. (It may serve parents well to think of how they teach children other skills: washing dishes, for example, or riding a bike.) Finally, recognizing that children are slowly acquiring skills reminds us of how important it is that parents model those skills themselves. If parents are asking children to handle frustration gracefully, parents must also ask whether and how they are doing that themselves.

Thinking in terms of this list of tasks minimizes the behavioral approach used by most parents in the US and other similar cultures. A behavioral approach—rooted in behavioral psychology—focuses primarily on extinguishing unwanted behaviors. It assumes that the child has the ability to choose differently and that she needs only exercise her will. It will probably make use of verbal reprimand or encouragement as a first step, but it assumes that those verbal interactions will ultimately be successful because they are reinforced by punishment. Introducing discomfort for the child will motivate her to avoid that suffering and make the desired change.

Each of the assumptions of the behavioral approach has significant limitations, though. First, the focus on extinguishing unwanted behaviors is too narrow and is entirely negative. It is an understandable focus, of course. Busy parents may find themselves paying most attention when children behave in ways that are inappropriate, problematic, or just annoying. In light of the larger horizon of apprenticing children to love, this is just shortsighted.

Second, a behavioral approach begins with the assumption that a child can choose differently, and that the parent's attention should be directed exclusively to bending the child's will. But this question has to be asked and answered carefully: *Can* the child simply choose differently? In some cases, she can. I myself have occasionally corrected one of my children with a short reminder: "You can do better than this." Parents who are tuned into a child's developmental stage and other key factors sometimes do know this to be true. In order to make that judgment, a number of questions have to be asked. Has the child acquired this skill at the level of mastery that the parents wish she had? Is the child acting primarily from a position of neediness or distress? (Is she tired or hungry or worried?) Anxiety, for example, often manifests itself in the form of opposition. Neurodivergence, mental health, and other individual factors mean that the question of each child's ability to satisfy a parent's requirements is a tricky one.

Third, a behavioral model rests on the strategy of introducing or threatening discomfort, and then leaves it to the child to moderate her behavior in order to avoid that discomfort. Unfortunately, this in and of itself does nothing to teach the hoped-for skill. It does nothing to reach the child's inner self, to inspire empathy or self-denial. In the worst cases, it can simply teach a child to avoid getting caught. Finally, for some children in distress, a promise of more discomfort simply won't have any effect. In our own family, our children who experienced complex trauma early in their lives often simply do not have the resources necessary to respond to this kind of threat. They are often too angry or anxious to care. The same can be true of any child.

Commitment to a behavioral model, one that rests ultimately on the threat of punishment, is not easy to let go. Isn't punishment just required in the most serious situations? For me, apprenticing children to love has always been most effective when I am allowing them to feel the love I have for them. John Bosco, renowned nineteenth-century priest and educator would agree: "Long experience has taught me that patience is the only remedy for even the worst cases of disobedience and irresponsiveness. . . . Sometimes, after making many patient efforts without obtaining success, I deemed it necessary to resort to severe measures. Yet these never achieved anything, and in the end I always found that charity finally triumphed where severity had met with failure. Charity is the cure-all though it may be slow in effecting its cure."[1]

The long view is the one required here, as well as the largest horizon. The goal of parents is not simply to manage behaviors but to lead their child toward maturity as a person. When we keep this in mind, we will encourage parents to prioritize love and connection with their children as the ground for all their interactions. As children grow and become more challenging, parents must continually return to the central posture described in chapter 1, one that parents often feel when their children are newborns: a posture of delight. That primary connection, and the commitment of unconditional love in which it happens, always comes first. Among all the other things they must be taught, children must be taught that, no matter what their behaviors, that connection itself is never threatened.

Thinking of the long term, and keeping in view this larger context of tender connection, makes it easier for parents to treat their children in a way that consistently reflects that reality. Even when they must correct, parents can adopt a stance of gentleness, respect, and compassion. Surely this is part of what Ephesians 6:4 means to communicate: "Fathers, do not provoke your children to anger, but bring them up with the training and instruction of the Lord."

But what would it look like to raise children beyond the narrow limits of the behavioral model, focused on acquiring the needed skills? We can deepen our consideration by looking briefly at each of the nine tasks listed above.

First, children must know what they want to do. Many parents will be tempted to respond to this first item with a wry smile and reassurance that *this* is not the problem for their child. It does make sense to begin here, though. To name and recognize desires is an essential element in learning the language of being human. The Christian tradition, moreover, does not teach that desire itself is a problem but rather that desires must be shaped by the ultimate goal of love. In situations where children's desires are simply ignored or minimized, real damage is done. For parents who feel like they are drowning in a child's desires—or perhaps even demands—two principles are important: Parents can simplify their children's environment so that they are not left awash in tantalizing options (something often accomplished quite intentionally, through the expert strategies of marketers). Kitchens can be stocked with foods that *are* allowed, for example, and advertisements offering a thousand new possibilities can be limited. When our children were very young, I often avoided bringing them into crowded grocery stores, where I knew I would say no to virtually every item that caught their eye, even if it meant shopping in the evening when they could be at home with their father. Each family will have to decide what makes most sense for them, but there is real wisdom in offering a simplified environment, rather than constantly trying to tamp down children's requests. Parents can also keep in mind that recognizing and naming desires does not require that the desires by satisfied. It is entirely possible to say, "I know you wish that you could have your friend's toy to keep. It's so much fun to play with. We have to leave it here, though."

Second, a child must learn to discern what is possible in any given situation. On this point, parents easily err in either direction. We can be too daring or overly timid. Again, parents tend to respond in a particular way: to react negatively when children attempt "too much." We hope that each child will find the balance that is right for her—and we don't want her to hesitate to try big things. A parent who is attentive and gentle will assist a child to fine-tune this skill.

Third, a child must learn to persist in the face of obstacles. If a child can find something she really wants to do, especially in the case of an ambitious undertaking, then she will have to find the perseverance to pursue it. Sometimes parents will not see the absence of this skill in young children as a pressing problem, but the challenge will become more obvious as children grow older and need this skill of persistence in order to pursue their goals, whether small or large. The importance of acquiring such a skill makes clear that parents engaging in the art of discipline cannot simply think of gaining compliance from their children as the ultimate goal.

Fourth, a child must acquire the ability to respond to requests from others. This skill actually includes several components. It means, for example, that the child must register that a request has been made, even when she is preoccupied. It also means that she must decide what her response will be. Finally, she must gather her energy to respond. Parents will do best if they remember that all these elements are strongly governed by the child's level of maturity. A delicate balance is at play. While parents may want to encourage a general stance of openness or willingness to cooperate, they will also want children to discern where they would do best to negotiate in response to a request, and also where they should simply say no.

All this focus on a child's self-determination may leave some parents confused and frustrated, and so it is important to include the fifth skill. Children must be able to exercise the trust in parents (and sometimes other adults) required to accede to requests and demands, even when those conflict with their own impulses. To many parents, this step may seem silly or superfluous. (Of course children can trust their parents, if the parents have been reasonably kind and caring!) It is important to consider things from the child's perspective here, though. Children live in a world where adults can sometimes provide things and can grant requests, and sometimes simply refuse to do that. (Why were they able to stop for an ice cream cone on the way home last Saturday but not today?) In this world, it can be very difficult to make sense of their parents' reasoning. Over time, it is crucial that children are able to recognize what it means to trust in someone who knows better than they do and whom they believe has their good in mind. This sort of trust in parents is very much like faith in God, which sits at the very center of the Christian life. It is in this context of trust that compliance is a desired trait. Even then, wise parents will look for opportunities to draw children into the reasons behind their decisions, where that is appropriate and possible. ("That ice cream was delicious, wasn't it? But today we have to get home quickly to make dinner.")

Sixth, a child must develop the ability to delay gratification and to forego an immediate reward in exchange for a longer-term good. This is a simple idea, but it is integral to many ways of acting in the world. In a sense, it is the heart of self-discipline. Ironically, this is best fostered not by harshness but in a context of trust. In order to sacrifice for a future good, a child has to have a firm sense that good things do lie ahead, and that their actions can function to bring about the outcomes they hope for.

Seventh, a child must develop the skill of maintaining emotional regulation, even in the face of frustration or disappointment. This is no small task. Remember, it is hardly surprising if small humans struggle significantly in getting their feet underneath them. There are many ways to maintain emotional regulation, and in truth, it simply comes more easily to some individuals. This is a skill where parents can significantly assist a child by beginning with empathy. It is also a dimension in which to be aware of the ways that children's brains and bodies are connected. A child who is tired or hungry will struggle much more with a disappointing no from a parent. A child who is in the midst of the turmoil of toddlerhood or the teenage years may be feeling off-balance in a chronic way, and may be much more susceptible to upsets that occur along the way. Trying to use a behavioral model is generally a disaster in the development of this skill. But there are options for parents. They can model regulation, and they can coach children who are struggling to find it. ("I know this feels hard right now. I'm so sorry. Let's just take a minute and then we will figure it out.") But even more, in the development of the skills of regulation, parents can actually share with children their own calm. Through what psychologists call "co-regulation," interactions with well-regulated parents can foster regulation in the child.

Eighth, as they practice all these skills, and as they see empathy modeled and directed toward them, children gradually develop empathy themselves. They develop the capacity to see the world from another's point of view, to respond with compassion to others' pain, and to celebrate others' joys. This skill is essential, but it is crucial to remember that it is a gradual developmental process. Expecting a three-year-old to share her toys out of concern for others is unrealistic. Over time, children *can* acquire this skill. As they do, they will become ready to take up their lifelong work of love.

Finally, children move toward the ultimate goal: coordinating all these skills in a way that allows them to step into the world as self-possessed, self-disciplined adults. Even then, growth will ideally continue in every one of these categories. Learning how to act effectively for the purposes of love is ultimately a lifelong task. Parents have the responsibility and the privilege of laying an essential foundation in a child's growing-up years—and of celebrating each small achievement along the way.

In the most immediate sense, this is work that only parents or other day-to-day caregivers can do. Other adults can support them by giving children some of the resources described here: examples of self-discipline, modeling, and coaching. A church community, in particular, can provide invaluable forms of support. In a community of faith, parents can find encouragement, including an atmosphere that confirms both the importance and the challenge of this parental work. They can be offered opportunities to connect with other parents so that they can support one another, and participate in conversations that allow discernment and problem-solving. Above all, if faith communities want to support parents, they can offer them a place where the parents themselves are immersed in a culture of gentleness and care. In apprenticing children to love, parents face a demanding, long-term undertaking. Nothing will benefit them more than a context in which they themselves are surrounded by love.

8

The Challenge of New Technology

Almost all parents are presented with challenges that their own parents did not face. When this happens, they cannot simply rely on the models they carry in their heads. They must start from scratch—and that can be difficult. We find ourselves in a moment in which this is true above all in one area: the use of new technologies.

How much screen time should parents allow young children? Should a sixth grader be given her own phone? These are important questions, but in a moment of significant social change, parents often feel caught short. In an environment of busyness and stress, they may well just make up the rules as they go along. It is not uncommon for parents to report both feelings of discomfort with their own practices and also a sense that it is impossible to carve out habits with which they feel more comfortable.

Screens are present to families in many forms—TVs, tablets, phones—and they offer resources that were hard to imagine only a few years ago. Children can find high-quality educational videos on virtually any subject. Grandparents who live far away can schedule a weekly video visit. Parents can organize a family movie night and watch an old favorite in only a couple of clicks.

At the same time, the presence of these screens brings real challenges and temptations. Making sense of them can help us navigate this new landscape with wisdom and calm, rather than vague unease. We must be aware that our brains—and our children's brains—interact with content on screens in a particular way. Put simply, it is very, very engaging. Some of this is just an intrinsic part of the technology: our eyes are drawn to light and movement. Bright colors, intriguing stories, immediate feedback in online interaction: these all cause brains to light up in satisfying ways. Increasingly, the satisfaction (technically speaking, the production of dopamine) is carefully engineered. Designers of social media, for example, self-consciously design "persuasive technology,"[1] using the best insights into human psychology to keep users engaged at maximal levels and for maximal amounts of time. Video games are designed precisely to make them difficult to walk away from. And smartphones allow all of these possibilities for engagement to be transported with the user wherever she goes. In all their forms, screens serve as sources of unusually rapid and powerful satisfaction. They demand attention, and they can crowd out forms of enjoyment that are slower, longer-term, and less intense, eventually weakening the capacity to attend patiently and to attend well. As prophetic thinker Marshall McLuhan's thought was once summarized, "We shape our tools and then our tools shape us."[2]

It is impossible to overestimate the value of the capacity of attention, a capacity that in most forms of interaction with screens is treated like a commodity to be harvested and sold to the highest bidder. In a sense, nothing is more basic to human beings than attending—and ideally, attending carefully and well. Whether we think of attending to those around us, to the world, or to ourselves, this is, in a sense, our most fundamental way of being present to, and engaging in, the life God has given us. Philosopher Simone Weil argues that prayer itself "consists of attention."[3] Prayer, she writes, "is the orientation of all the attention of which the soul is capable toward God. The quality of attention counts for much in the quality of the prayer."[4] If this is so, parents will surely want to think carefully about how to foster in their children this capacity.

What, then, can parents do in the face of the lure of the screen? Two fundamental strategies can help. First, parents can give careful thought and effort toward providing environments for their children in which screens are given a circumscribed place. Second, they can set up ground rules around screens that can function as guide rails for the whole family. With young children, a TV that is closed up in a cabinet and turned on only at certain times helps to set expectations for when it will be available. If parents simply create a rule for themselves that they will never hand a phone to a toddler in order to keep her occupied, they will find that battles over this possibility will be minimal. With older children, a family tradition might delay the ownership of smartphones at least until a child's fourteenth birthday, and even then, parents can choose phones with limited capacities. (Social media accounts, for example, should ideally be delayed even longer.) Parents can make clear that larger screens will never be located in children's bedrooms, and that all phones will be unavailable after a certain time at night. Family meals can be strictly device-free. Setting up expectations such as these does not mean that there will be no frustrations connected to screen use, but they do provide a starting place and make clear that screens always come with limits.

All of this is a lot of work for parents, and it can be tempting to consider just letting go and loosening up. Maybe creating so many limitations will only magnify their child's desire to find their way around them. The problem with this approach is that it forgets the engineering that has made screens so tempting. A comparison could be made here to highly processed foods, created precisely to override natural mechanisms indicating fullness. Just as parents often choose to limit the availability of these kinds of foods in their home, so they must limit screens. This focus on setting up a certain environment makes it possible for parents to monitor that environment, rather than monitoring children directly. The second of these options, monitoring children directly, is much more likely to create anxiety and conflict. Without ground rules in place, a parent may well grow uncomfortable with the length of time a child is watching screens and insist that "it's time to turn the TV off," but from the child's perspective, this will almost inevitably seem capricious.

The analogy to food can be helpful here and is worth expanding. One of the most essential responsibilities of a parent is to feed their children. If parents assume that interaction with screens is also an inevitable part of their children's lives, then they will ask questions and make decisions about how they want to offer various options. Most parents don't offer bags of potato chips for breakfast or set out large bowls of candy in the middle of the living room. In the same way, limiting screens—including access to the internet and social media—should be the norm from which parents begin. When dessert is available only after dinner, parents and children can both rely on that tradition, and parents will not end up micromanaging children's sugar consumption during the day.

Children can also be involved in these discussions once they reach their tween or teen years. Earlier, parents will simply make the decisions, but as children age, parents can invite their children, in small steps, to begin to assume the decision-making role. Eventually, children become adults who must manage their own screen time, and so the responsibility of parents is to coach and mentor them as they move into that role. One specific example might make sense with a child of twelve or fourteen, at which age a parent could ask: "What do *you* think is the maximum number of hours you should spend on screens each week?" Parents need not automatically accept the number the child gives, but they may also be surprised at the child's ability to step into such a conversation with careful thought. With the agreed-upon number of hours at hand, parent and child can then set up safeguards to remain within that limit. Parents can also take comfort in the idea that none of these specific rules or strategies need be absolute or permanent. Depending on the outcome of trying various strategies, reconsideration and renegotiation may well be required.

Beyond the general question of the extent of the presence of screens, a second concern has to do with specific content children might encounter on screens, whether in videos, video games, websites, social media, or elsewhere. Some of it—carefully filtered images of perfect faces and bodies—may not seem as dangerous at first, but over time they can create painful forms of self-criticism, especially for girls. Psychologists now speak about "Snapchat dysmorphia," which states that use of social media is linked to increased interest in cosmetic surgery. Other kinds of images and narratives are more immediately troubling: violence, graphic sexual content, and cruelty. The world of screens can create easy, and sometimes even unexpected, access to content that does children no good. We know the time-honored exhortation from Proverbs to "guard your heart, for everything you do flows from it" (4:23 NIV). What does it look like for parents in the age of screens to assist their children to follow that advice?

As with general access to screens, access to content must be discerned carefully. Full access to the internet, for example, is appropriate only in later stages of the teen years or young adulthood. Some parents may decide to block certain websites, including pornography, at the point of their internet router, so that *no one* using their Wi-Fi has full access to the internet. Two general strategies are available to parents: limiting content and monitoring content. Limiting content can involve a number of different options, including making it impossible to download apps or games without permission, excluding internet access, or allowing access but with various filters that screen out certain content. Monitoring is more complicated, but may sometimes be necessary. It may mean tracking a child's online activity or even checking text messages or app usage directly. Specific decisions about filtering and monitoring must be made by parents in the context of their knowledge of their own child and in the context of their relationship with that child.

In all of this, parents must strike a balance between vigilance and trust. It is simply not possible to guarantee with absolute certainty that a child will never have access to inappropriate content. Parents can be thoughtful and proactive, and then they can open up a dialogue with children that emphasizes cooperation in the task of guarding their hearts. Parents are the ones who will know best which children particularly exhibit impulsivity or feel a draw to what is dangerous, and they can adjust accordingly. In this area, it is perhaps more important than in any other that parents do what they must do all the time: set limits while also maintaining an ongoing conversation with their children, a conversation that includes explicit expressions of the love and concern that motivate them. This conversation is central not simply because of the way it allows for exploring, implementing, and analyzing limits but also for the correlated potential to continue to nurture that connection.

The counterbalance to the world of online content is a home that provides a rich environment of human connection, questions and ideas, and meaningful tasks. Some of these may actually include technology. At our house, for example, listening to audiobooks together has been a fruitful way to pass time, sometimes even while parents and children accomplish repetitive, tedious chores together. Parents will always have to keep an eye on their budget, but other resources are well worth investing in: art and craft supplies, musical instruments, a curated collection of books, favorite board games, and a kitchen that is available (within reason) for children to use. When a screen-free space is carved out, parents may be surprised at how eager children are to explore these options.

The final concern related to screens has to do with the way in which they can open children up to unhealthy forms of contact, whether with those they know or with strangers. Contact with individuals who are known most often stems from connections at school that then move to the online world through text messages or social media. The most damaging of these usually involve bullying of one kind or another. Bullying has always existed, of course, but as many have noticed in recent years, the relative distance and, in some cases, the anonymity involved in online interactions emboldens those who try to gain power by hurting others. This is another place where parents must be proactive. They can speak to their children about what bullying is and do everything possible to maintain ongoing communication about it. They can support and coach their children when they deal with minimal bullying, but when bullying is repeated or serious, they can take steps to close ranks with the school and other parents. Particularly between the ages of ten and sixteen, when children are beginning to establish new kinds of independence, it can be tricky for parents to discern exactly when and where to step in. The immediacy, speed, and potential reach of online communication means that parents often need to step in sooner in cases of online trouble than they would in the case of similar in-person situations.

Even more sinister encounters are also possible. The reality of online predators requires parents, especially parents with children between the ages of twelve and fifteen, to be alert to this danger. Parents should talk to their children both about online safety and about "red flags" to be aware of: contact with people with whom they have no in-person connections, inappropriate or intimate conversation, requests for explicit photos, and especially invitations to meet someone in person alone. Parents themselves should be alert for behaviors in their children that may signal a problem: a tendency to be obsessive or secretive about getting online, phone calls to or from people the parents do not know, the arrival of mail or packages from people the parents do not know, or a withdrawal from friends and family.

Sensitivity to all these dangers is indispensable, but as with other online challenges, parents can turn their attention toward positive alternatives. Above all, there is one antidote to the dangers of unhealthy online interactions: warm and stable connections with parents and other trusted adults. As I will argue in chapter 12, the years in which children may become more active online are also the years in which they are rightly becoming more independent, but that independence need not involve alienation from their parents. Parents may need to say out loud things they believe their child already knows: "You can come to me with anything. We can always figure it out together." "There is nothing you can do that would make me love you less." Parents must always make the best decisions they can about setting limits for their children, but they must also make space for real conversation and real relationship.

The model of parenting as apprenticeship always turns attention back to parents themselves: Are parents growing in the skills they hope to teach? Are they modeling them well? Nowhere is this more true than in relation to screens. The single most important thing parents can do is to begin by setting parameters for their own screen use. This may well be harder than it sounds. The same things that draw children to screens—entertainment, distraction, connection—draw their parents too.

As with the children, there is no reason to assume that a parent's use of new technologies is inherently problematic. The resources available to parents online are remarkable. And now, as numbers of parents are working from home, the task can become even more complicated. Is a parent standing in the kitchen reading an email from her boss setting a bad example? Or just getting done the work that has to get done? Some ground rules will likely help. Parents can be intentional about certain times and places where their phones are shut off. Times of transition and connection are particularly important: at dinnertime or at bedtime, for example. The principle for parents to keep in mind is this: it is very easy for time they spend on screens to expand to whatever limits are created. If they have no limits, their phones will likely be a constant presence in their lives—and the lives of their children. It is essential that in the ongoing work of using screens wisely and well, parents should begin with themselves.

What about the larger church community? Are there ways that parents can be supported in this complicated task? Much of what was said about discipline will apply here too. Parents need a village in which they can work these questions out. Parents of young children need support and ideas about how to manage several young children and when and how to include screens. Parents of young teenagers need information on particular safeguards and strategies. In addition to community wisdom, parents can get moral support. Perhaps the most difficult aspect of this challenge is that parents feel alone in deciding what is best and especially in enforcing limits. Having a community of like-minded parents who can support one another in making hard choices is an invaluable resource.

Beyond this, the church can offer families a genuine counterculture in which technology has its place but does not dominate. Social environments can be intentionally organized to be free of phones or other personal devices. Worship environments are traditionally places where screens are not present. Quiet, individual prayer can also be offered at regular times. Especially as communities discuss their issues openly, those in leadership may be surprised at the interest in opportunities such as a quiet retreat day, a "holy hour" involving Eucharistic adoration, or contemplative prayer services.

Navigating technology is no small undertaking. It requires energy and tenacity. As parents work together, and as parents invite their children into this work, it can be done well.

Parenting in Survival Mode

All families will have difficult days and difficult weeks. All will face challenging moments: a move, an illness, or a death in their extended family. A smaller number will face more significant crises: an accident, a serious diagnosis, or an extended period of unemployment. A handful of families will endure something truly catastrophic.

If there is any moment when parents can benefit from the accompaniment of the community around them, it is moments such as these. As painful as they are, these experiences actually become less traumatic in a context of support and compassion. Particularly when a crisis appears suddenly, families need to know there is someone they can reach out to immediately and feel confident that they will find a hand reaching back to them.

Many family crises are visible. We know how to respond when someone receives a troubling diagnosis or gets a phone call reporting a car accident. When we talk about family crises, though, it is good to remember that not all take this form. There is the layoff that only becomes a crisis as it extends over time. There are mental-health crises that are not as dramatic at first but gradually worsen and slowly pull a whole family into a confusing, dark spiral. For parents in particular, there can emerge a slow accumulation of the sense that a child is struggling without a clear picture of the causes. Not only mental illness but also complex medical situations, forms of neurodivergence, and other challenges can all fit this description.

Coming to understand what is going on and how to address it is actually a part of the burden of their experience.

For our family, this was very evident as one of our children was moving toward being diagnosed with anxiety. At one point, we actually had to call an ambulance for an alarming set of physical symptoms (later identified as a panic attack). Individual episodes would come and go, and it was only as the situation persisted and worsened that we ourselves were even able to name it as a "crisis." When the moment came that we enrolled our child in an outpatient program at a local hospital, I finally took a moment to send an email to a small group of trusted friends to tell them what had been going on and to ask for prayers. As it turns out, one of those dear souls immediately set to work and arrived at our house that evening with a dinner ready for us to eat. I received it with gratitude and a sigh of relief.

Those working in the field of mental illness actually sometimes call mental-health crises "no-casserole" illnesses because of the way that concerns about confidentiality—and, to put the matter more bluntly, shame—make it much less likely that those in crisis will receive a stream of well-wishes, prayers, and dinners like the one I eventually received. There are actually many sorts of no-casserole illnesses, and it is important that church communities find appropriate ways to be attentive to these as well. This chapter attempts to look at all of these sorts of crises together, to ask what parents in these situations need, and how these hard moments can be understood in theological perspective.

First, as I've already articulated, families need practical help, and sometimes they need it right away. This is a moment for churches to live out the model for their life together that they so often mention: they are a family. In the way that extended families are often ready to drop everything in a moment of crisis, churches must find a way to stretch and be present to those in need. At one time, this meant simply knocking on the door to say, "I'm here. What can I do?" In some communities, and in the context of some relationships, this might still be the ideal. But in a world of greater isolation and often of more virtual connection than physical, creative new forms of thinking are called for.

Online connections offer many new, and remarkably efficient, options. Email messages communicate to many recipients at once.

Websites can help organize delivery of meals and other kinds of help and can deliver updates. A parent who has little time and energy in the midst of a crisis might still be able to connect for a few minutes via videoconferencing to talk or pray with a small group. A weekly virtual meeting of this kind could make all the difference to parents feeling overwhelmed and isolated.

In-person support, however, is in many ways irreplaceable. "I'm here" is crucial, but it shouldn't stop there. Asking what help is needed is a good strategy. In many cases, however, parents facing a crisis are simply overwhelmed and unable even to formulate the list of what they need most. In these cases, specific, concrete offers can give them what they need.

"I would like to bring you dinner. Do you have any requests—or ingredients I should avoid?"

"I would like to pick up groceries or anything else you need. Could you send me a list—or would you rather I just bring some staples?"

"Would it help for me to watch the kids sometime this weekend?"

"Could I take the kids out to a movie (or some other activity)?"

"Could I come and do some cleaning for you? I know it's hard to let someone else do it, but I would love to give you that gift."

In many ways, it helps to think of these crises as a sort of recurrence of the newborn stage of parenting. A new baby is demanding, but the demands are something that can be predicted and anticipated. Parents of newborns expect that the increased burden is only temporary, and they operate according to a script they have seen acted out before.

In some ways, a family crisis requires much more help, and help of differing kinds. A crisis involving children increases the demands on parents, and parents, in turn, need immediate and tangible care themselves. In any of these crises, it makes most sense to think of the whole family unit as needing greater assistance and accompaniment from the outside.

Often in these situations, the suddenness, the confusion, and sometimes the sheer level of demand create new kinds of needs. As our family navigated the mental-health crisis described above,

I found myself saying that I was "off the map" of parenting as I knew it. Not only are these experiences demanding, but parents can sometimes struggle to even describe what is happening—to others or to themselves.

Second, families in crisis need not only practical support but also people who are able just to be present in a compassionate way to listen, both at first and in an ongoing way. This may well include those who are formally exercising their role as pastor, as well as others in the community. The crucial thing is that parents have an opportunity to speak about the difficulties they face and to find a listening ear. If practical needs are great, it will be especially important for those around them to seek out these moments, to indicate their availability, and to make clear that it is not simply an external situation but also a family's *experience* of that situation that matters.

Third, families need the kind of support that only the church can give. This will include prayers on their behalf and also opportunities for them to pray with others. It will include the concrete forms of anointing and other sacramental kinds of support. It will include something as simple as the offer of a hug at the church doors. Here again, any member of the community can step forward, although there is particular value in an ordained minister, in part because—at least in some traditions—only this person can represent the community as a whole. These concrete signs, sacramental and otherwise, really do matter. As I write, I am wearing a simple, woven bracelet. A friend has an infant granddaughter undergoing complex medical treatment, and another friend volunteered to make and then distribute these bracelets—including one for the worried grandmother—to a group of us as a reminder to pray and as a symbol of those ongoing prayers.

Responses like those described above can emerge in various ways. Some will be spontaneous and ad hoc. As mentioned in chapter 3, parents do best when they are already embedded in an active, larger community of support. This already creates an organic way for affected families to reach out for help or for others to notice that a crisis has appeared. Other families often have options for support that only they can give: offering childcare by hosting children in a familiar place with familiar playmates, or purchasing needed clothing, toys, or school supplies with a parent's practiced eye. Others can offer spontaneous support. Once, when I was organizing help for another family, I was deeply moved when an older gentleman at church stopped me, handed me a hundred dollars in cash, and asked me to use it "wherever it was needed most." And, of course, most importantly of all, prayer can be offered by everyone.

Churches will also want to consider programmatic ways to be available to families in crisis. Some have created a ministry specifically devoted to this kind of challenge, often functioning within a larger ministry to families. Advantages to this more organized approach are numerous. One is the way it allows some individuals to indicate a particular service they are ready to offer. One may keep frozen meals ready to deliver at a moment's notice; another may be able to step up not only to pray faithfully but to send messages of encouragement to the family.

Whether spontaneous or preplanned, support of these kinds will be invaluable to families walking through dark days. Something even more important, though, is essential. For families carrying a burden, especially a heavy or unexpected one, the greatest gift is a community in which their pain is welcomed with generosity and calm.

Christian communities often face the temptation to disregard or minimize pain as incompatible with a life of faith, even if unintentionally. For those in pain, a culture of this kind means that they struggle to find a place for their lived experience to land. They may find their sadness minimized, and they themselves may internalize this culture and do so themselves. A community that knows that pain and sadness are part of the life of faith is a place where families in crisis can gradually accept the reality of their story. Ultimately, of course, the Christian tradition affirms that every one of these crises will be woven into God's purposes of love. When and how that happens is often a mystery. The hope at the center of the gospel is not a protective shield against suffering in this life, and we do not serve Christ or Christ's people by brushing the pain aside.

The often-cited example of the friends of Job is relevant here. The book of Job offers a complex story in which God allows Satan to test Job, and Job then undergoes one form of grief after another. Three of Job's friends visit him in the midst of this mourning. For seven days, they simply sit quietly in solidarity with him. Then their tactics shift. They initiate a long and complicated dialogue in which they try to give an explanation for Job's suffering. Job, in contrast, merely affirms that he will continue to trust in God. In the end, all three friends are rebuked by God, whereas Job is praised. In moments of great grief and suffering, there is always a temptation to turn to explanation. Job offers another option: turning to one another in empathy and turning to God in trust.

The story of Job offers another evocative element, relevant for our consideration here. After praising Job and criticizing Job's friends, God is recorded as saying this: "So now take seven bulls and seven rams, and go to my servant Job, and sacrifice a burnt offering for yourselves, and let my servant Job pray for you. To him I will show favor, and not punish your folly" (Job 42:8). The suggestion here is not only that Job is commended for his faith in the midst of adversity but also that he will in a sense function as a priest, as a mediator of God's presence. What could this mean? Perhaps these families who are undergoing difficulties have a particular place and a particular function in their communities, a way that they reveal God's face.

In his first letter to the Corinthians, Paul makes a suggestion that I believe to be related. Having noted that the body of Christ has many members with many functions, all of whom need each other, he says this: "Indeed, the parts of the body that seem to be weaker are all the more necessary, and those parts of the body that we consider less honorable we surround with greater honor" (1 Cor. 12:22–23). Paul's words are not usually applied to families who are in crisis, but we could consider them in this context. Where there is a temptation to see only weakness or "tragedy," Paul's words suggest that families in these situations deserve to be particularly honored. Paul, after all, is the one who spoke of his own experience of what he called a "thorn in the flesh," a kind of weakness through which he received this message from God: "My grace is sufficient for you, for power is made perfect in weakness." Paul summarized with this paradox: "When I am weak, then I am strong" (2 Cor. 12:7, 9–10).

This insight does not mean that we romanticize suffering, and certainly does not mean that we seek it out. It means that suffering is not ultimately an enemy who can undo us. It means that, as we rely on Christ and seek out his strength, weakness can also be a gift.

Families who need extra support serve to remind all of us of our finitude and teach us not to despise dependency. They challenge us to loosen our grip on efficiency, productivity, and self-sufficiency. In particular, if we are focusing on parenting, they remind us that we are never as much in control of our lives as we imagine we are. They ultimately give the larger community a new opportunity to love.

In the end, we may even be able to share this understanding with them. For me, one of the greatest gifts in hard moments has been friends who have said, "Thank you for letting us help. We love you, and we are glad and grateful to have the chance to be with you through this."

And for parents, finally, these moments are profound opportunities to parent. If parents apprentice their children in the art of life, then suffering will inevitably be a part of that. For children to be cared for tenderly when they are the most needy, for children to see their parents receiving care from others, and for children to know that love can see them through even the hardest moments: these are inestimable gifts.

10

Parents—and More Than Parents

To describe parenting as a vocation is to recognize both its dignity and its profound importance. In the end, what could be more consequential than taking a human being by the hand and leading her all the way from infancy to adulthood? Once they take up this work, moreover, parents usually become more aware of how finite that time period is, and of how quickly it goes. As the author of one parenting book has noted, between the day a child is born and the time she turns eighteen, parents get 940 Saturdays.[1] On a child's fifth birthday, 260 of those Saturdays are already gone.

Awareness of the importance and the urgency of this task can also have unfortunate consequences. Especially when it is combined with the relative isolation of nuclear families already discussed in chapter 3, it can leave parents completely swallowed up in this work. The more dedicated they are to the task at hand, the greater this danger becomes.

A parent who is thinking only of the vocation of parenting is losing track of the larger Christian account of vocation. Every individual vocation, or calling, is built on the single central calling of baptism. Before God calls a person to any particular task or any particular role, God gives this more primary call to be reconciled through Christ and enfolded in the larger purposes of God's saving, healing work. Before anything else, God invites each of us to know ourselves as beloved and to enter into a relationship of intimacy and trust with God through Christ. Jesus sums it up in speaking to his followers in John 15:15: "I have called you friends."

Every individual calling, then, including parenthood, is grounded in something bigger and deeper than itself. And over the span of the long task of raising children, this deeper grounding must be attended to—and sometimes, revived. Ironically perhaps, this recognition of a larger context often helps parents to be the best parents they can be. In the simplest sense, it can replenish a parent for the work they do with their children. In a deeper sense, it reorients the entire project. It is easy to imagine that children are a product that parents are producing. In this view, children's behavior ratifies or discredits their parents' efforts. Their children's accomplishments are, with hardly any gap at all, their own. Parenting grounded in the larger call of baptism, though, is something else. It is rooted in the larger purposes of love, and every satisfaction, every disappointment, every moment of fatigue is referred back to *those* purposes. Parents are, of course, in relationship with their children, but it is not the children who have called them to the work, and it is not the children's task to encourage or to praise or to justify. Ultimately, it is by grace, grounded in the love of God and immersed in the communion of the Holy Spirit, that parents find solid ground. Parenting of this kind is a call to love from one's own deepest reality of having been loved.

There are several practical ways in which parents can recognize and live this broader reality, and can find what they need to live it out. First, parents must find ways to truly rest. I say this realizing just how difficult it can be to accomplish. In our family, we will spend at least thirty years raising five children (so far!). Both my husband and I have been either full-time students or full-time employees for virtually all those years, and none of those years have brought us into proximity with extended family. There have been some very, very long days. But there have been some possibilities that have served us. We have prioritized opportunities for each of us individually to step away for socializing or recreation. We have found good friends with whom we can relax with all our children present or with whom we can trade off childcare so that each couple gets a little downtime. This sort of cooperative initiative can actually take many different forms: some parents create a sort of supper club where, for example, five families join together so that each of them cooks enough for all, but only on one day of the workweek.

However provisions are made, these forms of rest are most fruitful when they are woven regularly into the fabric of daily and weekly life. Parents who are home full time with children might take Saturday morning as a time away from the house and children. A monthly girls' night out, especially when it includes time for real conversation, can have tremendous effect.

Second, parents need opportunity for real friendship with those other than their spouses. These relationships can take many forms: they might be one-on-one or they might occur in the context of a group. They might be friendships with other parents, which offer obvious forms of camaraderie, or they might connect parents to those in very different life circumstances, where there are also particular benefits. Friendships connecting parents to their lives before their children arrived and friendship connecting them to others who are older or have more life experience, even when they require more intentionality, are often well worth the effort.

Third, even if it can happen only in small doses, parents need opportunities to learn and grow and to express creativity. Many simple hobbies—reading, gardening, or music-making—can serve this purpose, but for exhausted parents, they are often crowded out by time spent on screens. As is often true, mindless engagement with screens can be easier in the moment but less satisfying in the long term. (Of course, as noted in chapter 8, on-screen activities that are pursued intentionally can provide many benefits.)

Fourth, parents need opportunities for exercise, for time spent in green spaces, for activities that are physically invigorating and restorative. This category is intentionally a broad one. It would perhaps be ideal for every parent to have several outings a week to take a long, uninterrupted hike in a forest, to swim at the pace that leaves them happily worn out, or to bike along a beautiful, safe path. When these options are not available others can also offer some of the same benefits. A walk in the neighborhood or on a treadmill or even just a short time spent in a park or other green space can be invaluable. Here again, cultural factors can work against parents. In a car culture, caregivers for young children can easily spend the whole day indoors if outdoor spaces are not particularly hospitable and driving the children somewhere is more trouble than it is worth.

Finally, although spirituality can be a part of everything mentioned above, parents also need opportunities for spiritual grounding and growth in activities like organized prayer, Bible study, adult formation events, and retreats. In some cases, these opportunities might be particularly focused on parents. I myself was immensely enriched over the course of several years by an annual mothers' retreat offered through our children's school. Traveling to a retreat house for a weekend gave us all the quiet and calm we craved. Talks were focused on themes of general interest, such as hope and forgiveness. The fellowship over meals and around the fireplace in the evening was unique. In that setting, we were able to be transparent and vulnerable with one another in new ways, to offer one another advice and encouragement, and to pray together with a profound sense of solidarity.

Parents can be encouraged and supported in pursuing spiritually nourishing options on their own or with friends as well. Recently a small prayer group of friends has been a lifeline for me. We have not attempted anything ambitious. We meet every couple of weeks or so in one of our homes to share concerns and pray together. Occasionally we include a glass of wine or appetizers. Once or twice we've celebrated a birthday with a special dinner out. It happens that we are all mothers, but the task of mothering is not the only topic raised. Above all, these gatherings give us a moment to breathe, to remind ourselves of the deepest realities in which our lives are rooted, and to join our prayers in supporting one another. Occasional texts asking for prayer throughout the week have become a natural outgrowth of our regular meetings.

Like our prayer group, not all such opportunities need be focused on parents or parenting in particular. The most basic movements of faith—rediscovering ourselves in God's love, reorienting ourselves in God's forgiveness, and re-centering ourselves in God's grace—are crucial for both parents and nonparents alike. But as this chapter suggests, recalling their deepest identity in relationship with God is indispensable for parents who are tempted to think of themselves only as parents, and only in terms of the many tasks they must complete.

One further word that applies particularly to parents and their spiritual lives may be in order here. Given the demands of parenting, and the many ways in which parents turn their attention to their children, parents and those ministering to them may come upon something unexpected. In all of the busyness of their lives, even and perhaps especially for parents whose busyness includes church activities, stopping to attend to the state of their own hearts may be a shock. In short, that inner space may seem oddly empty. Parents may find that when they are not engaged in faith-related activities with and for their children, they have a hard time mustering motivation at all. They may find that they have new questions about the faith or new doubts, but when they already have so much to which they must attend, and when they are already in the process of handing on the faith to their children, where would they find room to attend to any of this? Perhaps we should not be surprised that this can be a difficult moment.

What to do in the face of such a crisis is never simple, but for parents an interesting possibility emerges. In chapter 5 we spoke about three of the most essential realities into which children are apprenticed: joy, purpose, and connection. As noted there, these are the grounds on which a living faith can take hold. Before responding by simply redoubling efforts to attend church or to pray, we might begin by asking where weary parents specifically need to be rooted again in these essentials. The ways to reclaim them are not always direct, but there are winding paths that do tend to lead there.

- Simplicity is a way to joy, and parents often need the simplest opportunities to hear God's voice again, whether in the form of a long walk or a quiet hour of adoration.

- Gratitude rejuvenates a tired soul. Simply speaking or writing words of gratitude can be unexpectedly effective. Journaling focused on gratitude often helps create focus in the midst of fatigue.

- When they are directly involved with their children, parents look for opportunities to reorient their time, wherever possible, toward play. (Any parent who has spent a summer evening playing in the sprinkler and eating finger foods for dinner knows the way it can lighten the load.) Bringing moments of lightheartedness back into the day-to-day of parenting can unexpectedly reorient the whole parenting task to joy.

• An older adult who will serve as prayer partner and mentor is perhaps the greatest single gift to a parent struggling with faith.

In the largest sense, parents can begin to move toward what a seventeenth-century Carmelite friar named Brother Lawrence called "the practice of the presence of God." In his classic book by the same name, Brother Lawrence details the way in which every small action of the day can be transformed as one becomes aware of God's presence. Every task can be a form of surrender to God's will and can be an act of love done for him. Short prayers that are repeated throughout the day—"Help me to love as You love" or "Jesus, I trust in You"—are simple ways to create and maintain this prayerful focus. Once I was talking with the head of my children's school, a sister in the Dominican order, and she and I were commiserating about how challenging life seemed to be for both of us at that moment. She told me that as various crises and challenges arose, especially as the demands seemed more than she could manage, she had taken to having a sort of unbroken conversation with God. Knowing that she could do only one thing at a time, she would turn from her most recent task and ask simply, "What next, Lord?" These small prayers may not seem like much, but living each moment consciously in God's presence is, in the end, the only way to keep the command of 1 Thessalonians 5:17 to "pray without ceasing."

If we think of parenting as a kind of apprenticeship, it makes sense to imagine that parents must continue to practice actively the skills they hope to teach. If joy, they must practice joy. If an abiding sense of purpose, they must experience that sense in their own hearts. And if faith is the center around which all of life moves, then parents must have the space and encouragement they need to continue, as Philippians 2:12 says, to "work out [their] salvation."

11

Busy Days

On any given day you can find thousands of families of school-aged children making their way through an incredibly demanding schedule. The morning routine means getting up and getting moving for the whole household, often juggling bathrooms, backpacks, and hopefully a bit of breakfast. One or two parents head off to separate workplaces, and three kids can easily mean three different schools (or daycare). Afternoons are activities, rehearsals, and lessons—and various arrangements of after-school care. Dinnertime may well be a drive-through meal on the way from one stop to the next, and evenings are for household chores, homework, and maybe another program or practice. For some parents, economic demands mean a "second shift," where, in one way or another, they go back to work in the evenings. In all cases, parents end up eventually falling into bed only to start all over again the next morning.

As parents move into the "middle years" of parenting, it is very easy for life to become this kind of busy blur. Parents never set out to create such a demanding life, but as balls are thrown at them, they try to catch them and begin juggling school, sports, music, clubs, church activities, and more. They are not doing anything very different from other families around them. Somehow, in the end, every moment is spoken for. Parents certainly find little time for themselves or their marriages or the kind of spiritual rejuvenation discussed in chapter 10. Both parents and children are tired and anxious.

We don't always notice it, but smartphones have made it even easier to be thrown in a dozen different directions. In the past, prearranged commitments—like a family dinner at a certain time—might have functioned more as a kind of limit. Now, when family members can reach one another by text or see one another on various tracking apps, they may be even more likely to be in different places throughout the day.

Of course, being in different places can happen in varied ways. Both for parents and children—especially as children begin to move into adolescence—screens can draw even people who are sitting in the same room to very different places. In chapter 8 we talked more about screens, and in chapter 12 we will talk more about the early adolescent years. For my purposes in this chapter, I want to note that in these busy middle years, screens can be one of the factors that draw children away from parents, and that draw all members of the family into a dizzying stream of activity that they may not have intentionally chosen.

If we think of parenting as apprenticeship, questions arise immediately. In this frenzy, where is the opportunity for apprenticeship? Or, we could ask a different question: To what are parents apprenticing their children? Parents need to ask carefully what is driving all this activity. Is it a hope to excel in particular skills? Is it a general, unnamed drive for productivity? Is it just the result of so many options presenting themselves? For some parents, financial demands mean they must work long hours. For others, however, the long hours could better be seen as a choice, required more by wants than by needs. Whatever their particular situation, this is a place where parents will have to do the hard work of thinking carefully and of saying no to some of the possibilities that arise.

In another dimension of what is perhaps the same dynamic, these years can bring a constant stream—not of activities but of possessions! When a new baby arrives, many parents are taken aback at the long lists of what they should, or could, acquire. In the case of a new baby, the crib and high chair can also provide some sense of comfort as they take on what feels like an enormous task. Ten years later—as sometimes becomes painfully obvious in a move from one home to another—the amount of "stuff" exceeds what parents ever could have imagined. Clothes, toys, electronics, gadgets: they seem almost to multiply on their own. And stuff then creates its own demands for management and upkeep and storage. As more than one observer has noted, "The stuff we own ends up owning us."

In both cases—busyness and belongings—comparison with other families usually does not help. Such comparison has always existed, but in an age of social media, the effect can be constant. Proud parents often post the happiest moments of children's achievements, and it can leave us with the impression that constant success is to be expected. In the same way, a stream of images of perfect homes and perfect families (arrayed in matching clothing and laughing joyfully) can gradually but firmly reset our sense of "normal." The images are all beautiful, but the desire to re-create them can cause a constant restlessness and endless to-do lists.

Even more important is that question of what gets left out. In a constant stream of activities, distractions, and possessions, are there ways that our children have the opportunity to practice things like compassion, community, rest, and play? If generosity is packaged into a holiday food drive or curiosity is represented only in a field trip to the museum, can we say that our children are truly living these realities? Or are they simply checking off boxes?

For parents in the midst of busy days, what is the answer? In recent years we have begun to see more families making choices that point to a different way. Increasing numbers of families are choosing to homeschool, and many report that the possibility of simplifying their schedule is a big factor in their decision. Some give away most of their belongings to move into a "tiny house" or even into a recreational vehicle. Even though these are choices that may not be desirable or even possible for all families, they help remind us that parents may well need to make decisions that seem radical or countercultural.

I have watched with admiration as a number of our friends have made these kinds of decisions. One family lives in a rural setting, with Dad's woodworking shop only a few steps from the house. As their oldest children have begun to marry and have their children, they continue to have a profoundly rich family culture and sense of "home." Another family has lived as missionaries, teaching their children in the most effective way possible that "home" is a reality tied to hearing God's voice and answering. A third family lives in a busy urban setting in a larger community that shares a large house. Their community often welcomes guests, as well, and their children are learning all the ways in which commitment and connection are not limited to their nuclear family. All three have reminded me that when it comes to parenting and family life, there is no requirement to do what "most people" are doing.

For most families, the choice will likely be something that is very difficult: to remain in the situation in which they find themselves while also finding ways to live out a sense of simplicity and purpose. Above all, parents need the opportunity to step back and reflect—not just once but regularly. Where *do* they want to live? What relationship to a neighborhood and community do they envision? How will they structure the days, weeks, and seasons of their family life? Some of these will be big decisions, but the power of small practices and habits should not be overlooked.

Our family was able to make several decisions that provided some measure of sanity. When our children were still young (and only the oldest two had begun school), homeschooling was an option that made sense for us. It allowed us to prioritize our family and spend time together in a way that would have been impossible if we had gone the alternate route: driving our two oldest children to two different schools. Then, during the next phase of our family's life, we were able to live only a block away from the K–8 school that all five of our children attended. Buying that house was a stretch financially, but we could see the ways in which it would simplify our life. During the years they attended the school, our children were only a three-minute walk from home. Bringing a forgotten lunch box to school was a simple matter, and other activities that happened at school, from social events to athletics to Boy Scouts, were easier to manage. On several fronts, when considering options for individual children, we asked about the impact on our *family*. We wanted to give our children opportunities, and sometimes we stretched in order to do that, but we also wanted to give our children a family life with calm at the center, and that sometimes required saying no.

Every family will have to engage in their own discernment on these questions. As the examples above suggest, the answers for individual families may differ widely. For Christian families, this kind of discernment happens best when it grows out of a larger Christian community. This could include pastors, extended family, close friends, or a community of like-minded parents formed at church or some other Christian community. In this process of discernment, the fundamental agreement matters: these are conversations that are most fruitful when they are rooted in the sense of parenting as a vocation, and the deeper rooting in the call to be a follower of Jesus Christ. They also are most fruitful in the context of what we might call "thick ecclesiology"—a recognition of church not simply as one community in which families participate but as the central reality that grounds their lives. Christian families are rooted in the larger reality of the church, and just as individuals work out their own vocations in that context, families can benefit from seeking the shape of their familial life with awareness of that larger reality. Families who engage in mission work are an explicit example of this, but there are as many possibilities of achieving this as there are families.

In our own family, we came to feel early on that we were called in particular to exercise hospitality. In a certain sense, we have thought of our own role as parents as a form of hospitality. (This is actually true for every parent, but as adoptive parents, we may have had an easier time keeping it in view.) We have looked for ways to invite others in as well. Our practice of eating dinner as a family has made it easier to include one or two more, even sometimes at a moment's notice. The house I mentioned earlier was a financial stretch in part because it is large, but its size has created the possibility for inviting people in regularly: for the evening, for the weekend, or sometimes for much longer stays. Over the years, this has created a sense of purpose that has guided us. In other families, different habits and practices will likely be emphasized, but each family has to look for a broader sense of purpose that will allow for wholeness and holiness.

No matter what individual charisms they feel called to exercise, there are certain ideals that all families must honor if they are to find wholeness. First, in a busy 24/7 world, families have to create their own practices of rest and reflection. I have mentioned a couple times that the family dinner table has been an anchor for us. We have also looked for ways to honor Sunday as the Lord's Day. This is a day for church, for rest, and for family. It has not always been easy, and youth sports leagues especially have sometimes made it difficult for us, but we have worked hard to avoid allowing Sunday to become just another day. Other practices have varied considerably. For several years, for example, my husband and I were able to make Sunday evenings a time for unhurried conversations about family matters. Even as we took up varying practices, keeping the goals of rest and reflection in view pushed us to continue to look for options.

Second, in a world of appearance and accumulation, parents will have to be intentional about cultivating a culture of simplicity and generosity. There are endless possibilities. We know more than one family who follows the rule of three Christmas gifts. Citing the fact that Jesus himself received only three gifts, parents offer children "something they want, something they need, and something to read." Other families may vary the formula slightly, or grandparents may arrive with another gift, but the basic principle stands: in limits we find freedom.

Involving children in giving generously to others can at times be even more challenging. In our family, we were sometimes able to bring our children to a meal kitchen on the weekends. At one small shelter we were able to cook and serve breakfast as a family one Saturday a month. Even more significant are situations where families' lives are woven together with those they are serving. A small example in our own household is that when we have guests, our children sometimes wait on them, serving food or removing dirty dishes. Again, there is no one-size-fits-all solution that will work for every family, but keeping the ideal of apprenticing to simplicity and generosity will make a difference.

So much of what we are discussing here will be the work of individual parents in individual families. But is there any role for pastors or a church community to play? There certainly is. To begin, just one brief note that could perhaps be perceived as negative but is nonetheless important: pastors and others in church leadership can begin by keeping everything here in mind—and by consulting often with parents—to be sure they are not overscheduling family-oriented events. They might also consider whether, in addition to children's activities, women's groups, and so on, there might be fruitful ways to include the whole family. At our family's parish, for example, Mother's Day is always marked with a parish dance in the gym, where you can find everyone from the youngest to the oldest celebrating together. More positively, churches should not be hesitant to speak about the need for countercultural choices to be made. It is not uncommon for churches to address more traditional concerns: vices, like selfishness or pride, or concerns with violence or pornography. These are real concerns, and it is important to witness unapologetically to another way. Sometimes, though, the less obvious and more pervasive dynamics must be engaged as well. Among many others, there are two principles that will be especially important here.

The first is the tradition of sabbath rest. I mentioned above our own family's commitment to Sunday rest, but this is a larger theological principle that deserves a central place. Sabbath rest is not simply a rule about what should not be done on Sundays. It is an invitation to step out of the endless cycle of productivity, to embrace dependence on our Creator, and to place trust in God in a habitual, concrete, embodied way. In focusing simply on rest in God, it offers a way to practice for eternity in God's presence. It is given a central place in the creation narrative and in the Ten Commandments, so shouldn't we also treat it as central?

The second is the conviction that all our possessions are given to us not simply to possess but to steward. When all our belongings are simply our own, the cycles of acquisition, organization, and decluttering become endless, as we constantly try to arrange things according to our own vague sense of satisfaction or convenience. When we recognize that all we have is actually given to us to manage for God's purposes, everything appears in a new light. We are more likely to begin in wonder for everything with which we are entrusted. We are more likely to begin in gratitude when we find we are able to meet our family's basic needs. After that, the way we make use of possessions is suddenly a task flung wide open. We hold to things less tightly, as we ourselves are drawn into larger purposes of compassion, creativity, and love.

Finally, as is true with other tasks of parenting, the church can look for ways to facilitate community and conversation among parents who are working these things out. Considering the questions together, in an atmosphere of prayer, can yield valuable insights. Even more, parents who are able to live within a larger community of like-minded parents will find new practical possibilities. A co-op of toys and books and clothing allows each family to buy less. Sharing large, family-friendly meals and fellowship can be a particularly rich way to truly rest a bit (especially if the menu is a simple one). And families can also cooperate in reaching out. In our own neighborhood, one small group of families often gathers at Christmastime to sing carols at a local nursing home. In many ways, the ideals of simplicity and generosity really work best in a larger context of community.

Forging a different way forward is possible, even if it is not always easy. When we begin with an awareness of the ways that we are already sustained by God's generous love, when we are able to rely on God—and on others around us—a whole new world appears.

12

Moving into Adolescence

Parenting tweens and early teens can be the toughest of all the phases of parenting. Children are suddenly tall. They are suddenly self-conscious. They are suddenly complicated and moody. Parenting strategies that worked well six months earlier now go nowhere. Is it any wonder that parents often look ahead to this season with trepidation?

These years of early adolescence are often compared to toddler-hood—and with good reason. Like a two-year-old, a twelve-year-old finds herself in possession of new strengths and abilities, and a new desire to use them. Like a three-year-old, a thirteen-year-old may also be confused and frustrated by parents and others who do not seem to recognize how capable she is. Adolescents experience a new desire for autonomy. At the same time, the sudden changes leave the child herself off-balance and struggling to manage big emotions. Parents may even see similarities in the way an individual child moves through toddlerhood and early adolescence, as both leave her navigating new developments and new uncertainties.

In early adolescence, significant growth is happening in several ways. Tweens and preteens experience marked cognitive development, as brain development creates new possibilities. Development in the frontal lobe of the brain allows a surge in abstract thinking, the ability to analyze ideas, recognize patterns, and synthesize information beyond what is observed physically. Development in the frontal lobe cannot always keep up with growth in the amygdala, the part of the brain associated with emotions, impulsive behavior, and aggression. So a thirteen-year-old may suddenly be able to solve complex math problems (in a way that parents struggle to remember and keep up with!). At the same time, in everyday situations, she is more likely to rely on the amygdala more than the frontal lobe and so to act suddenly, without taking all the relevant factors into consideration and without the same concern for larger context and long-term implications. Is it any surprise that adolescence is often a time for risk-taking that can leave parents gasping? The amygdala is also connected in important ways to patterns of psychological reward, so during early adolescence, we often see increased reward-seeking and novelty-seeking, as well as an increased need for social and environmental stimulation.

The social dimensions are especially important. As children move toward greater autonomy, they naturally rely less on parents for direction. At the same time, the esteem of their peers grows in importance. In all relationships, new possibilities appear, as abstract thinking creates new avenues for empathy. All this inevitably creates two related possibilities: the capacity for intense—and intensely meaningful—relationships, and, at the same time, the inevitability of disappointment and heartbreak when and where relationships do not proceed as hoped.

Tied to all of this is physical and sexual maturation. New levels of hormones, for example, are tied directly to the development of the amygdala. A rich and complex sense of self, connected both to sexuality and gender, is suddenly in play, and is only slowly worked out over the coming years. In connection with the kinds of brain development described above, it is easy to see how the appearance of sexual desire in all its many forms, from flirtation to challenging social maneuvering to intense longing, can catch the young teenager herself as off-guard as it does her parents. It is also easy to see the wide range of reactions it can provoke. Young teenagers have a particular capacity to fall head over heels in love; parents of young teenagers have a particular capacity to note the appearance of new kinds of sexuality in connection with new kinds of impulsivity and risk-taking and take account of all the dangers.

There may be no other moment of parenting that is as poignantly fraught. Parents are right to be concerned as they watch their children step into this new world. Adolescents, on the other hand, have their own perspective: it is their own project, their own lives, that are at stake, and not primarily those of their parents. Perhaps nowhere does it become obvious that adolescence involves a new sense of self. Children this age have memories of earlier years, of course, but they generally have a strong sense that they, as agents in the larger world, are just emerging. The fundamental question for parents is whether they can welcome this very different form of "taking first steps," not allowing caution to become a kind of anxiety or their understandable concern to cloud a deeper sense of joy in this new phase of their child's life.

In taking stock of early adolescence, it is important to note that this is the season when mental illnesses are most likely to emerge. Anxiety disorders are the most common, with recent estimates suggesting that more than a third of teens struggle with anxiety in a way that significantly interferes with their life. In the long term, there is good news. If they get the support they need, most young people will be able to manage their mental health as they move into adulthood and the tumult of adolescence fades. In the meantime, anxiety itself and the strategies that young teens use to try to manage it can be unnerving for their parents.

The challenge of mental illness underscores a broader dynamic that emerges with adolescence and makes parenting much more difficult. As children grow older, as their problems sometimes become bigger and scarier, and as the child's own sense of privacy becomes apparent, parents often have to consider questions of confidentiality when discussing their children's needs. This can lead them to a place of isolation just at the moment they most need solidarity and support. Parents of toddlers don't hesitate to gather and discuss the ups and downs of potty training, benefiting from the shared wisdom and the camaraderie those conversations provide. Discussing a child's emerging sexuality is not always as simple.

What are parents to do? The demands of this early adolescent period are very real, and they can feel overwhelming. The first step, perhaps, is to note the crucial importance of parenting during these years. As children move into adolescence, they do not need less parenting. They need parenting of a different kind. In the face of confusing behaviors or even hostility and resentment, parents must not pull back but should lean in—although now in significantly different ways. The goal now is not primarily to direct but rather to engage, to accompany, to befriend. In some ways children in their tweens and early teens need their parents more.

What will these new forms of parenting look like? There are a number of crucial elements. First, parents must shift to being present in a different way. When children are younger, parents are more active: supervising, clothing, feeding. In this new phase, parents must also find ways to be present and available in a way that allows for kids to take the lead. In our own family, my husband has a habit of sitting and reading in such a way that he is easily visible and can be interrupted. As it turns out, throughout their teen years our children have been happy to interrupt. Sometimes it is just to report a problem or request transportation, but other times it is to share an experience or ask a question. My husband usually ends up saying very little. But that passive sort of availability is a crucial element in allowing the encounters to occur. Driving together can also be an opportunity for these kinds of conversations. Leaving space for this possibility is just one of many reasons to delay or limit the availability of smartphones for early teens.

Second, parents must practice new kinds of conversational skills. It is easy for parents to fall into giving advice or reminding their children of the "right answers." It is easy to offer their own opinions on a wide variety of topics. What young teenagers need is someone who will listen first. A posture of empathy is crucial here. What is important to the child herself? What is she feeling and thinking about the things she reports? For many parents, there is real value in practicing specific scripts that remind them to focus in this way:

"That sounds pretty frustrating/disappointing/confusing."

"It makes sense to me that you feel . . ."

"Tell me more about that . . ."

"Do you know what you're going to do next?"

"Are you looking for help in solving this, or do you just want to talk it through?"

This is not always easy. Parents need significant skills in self-awareness, especially when they have strong reactions to what they are hearing. But this kind of patient attention gives children the space they need to know what they feel and think, and it fosters in them habits of discernment and mastery. In the end, parents must not simply attempt to share their insights with their children but foster and celebrate in the children themselves the skills that allow them to arrive at insights of their own.

This is not to say that a parent can never offer opinions or share her experiences, of course. At the right moment, it can create a sense of solidarity for children to hear stories in which their parents struggled or learned something important. Broader principles can also be articulated. Children want to know that advice is being offered by someone who sees the situation, who sees what is at stake for them, and who stands beside them and not simply over them.

Third, parenting tweens and teens means giving children more room as they make decisions. Of course, there are limits to put in place (more on that below). This fundamental truth applies, though: children cannot move into adulthood if parents try to make it *impossible* for them to make any mistakes. If this feels risky, that's because it is. At the very least, it means that children may do things that their parents believe are shortsighted or foolish or in some other way less than ideal. The dangers in the other direction are just as great, however. Children, sensing that their parents do not trust them, may never learn fully to trust themselves. Or, having lived in an overly controlled environment, they may struggle when they have to navigate the world on their own. Here it is important to remember the end goal of the apprenticeship process: an adult. It can help for parents to imagine themselves as coaches. A coach pours a great deal into her players. She gives them whatever she thinks will equip them to succeed. But she cannot follow them out onto the field and play the game for them. If she were to do that, they would never really learn to play, and any victory would ultimately belong not to them but to her.

Christians, who think of God as a parent, will find a model for this kind of parenting in God's own actions. God does not coerce but rather loves and leads in a way that fully exercises the free will of human beings. God allows mistakes. Most importantly, God's actions show that mistakes can be moments for growth and learning and can be woven into the purposes of love. We could think of the story of Israel's demand for a king in 1 Samuel. God is described in this text as believing the Israelites are making a mistake (their choice amounts to a rejection of God). God allows it, though, and commands the prophet Samuel to anoint a king. It is no surprise that many things go wrong in the monarchy of Israel, but from one king, David, described in 1 Samuel 13:14 as a "man after [God's] own heart," God begins to weave good. In the end, God will redeem the category of the "King of the Jews" in completely unexpected and radically life-giving ways.

Fourth, closely related to the freedom to make mistakes is another gift that fledgling teens need from parents: consistent encouragement and support. Teens need parents who celebrate their newfound competence and independence. Even (and perhaps especially) when they brush them off, children need parents who are their biggest fans. The victories may be large and public or small and hidden. Parents' support may be showy or it may be quiet. At heart, children need to know that their parents see and take joy in the ways they are growing.

None of this means that parents must abandon their role of creating limits or requirements. As younger children do, young teens actually gain a sense of security from a framework in which their parents communicate clear expectations. What is essential is that this framework is one that is founded in respect. Where parents of a younger child might simply announce a screen-time limit, parents of a tween or teen might sit down to talk through the challenge, looking for the possibility of collaborating to create a plan for screen limits on which everyone agrees. In this new phase, parents will be even more open to countersuggestions and creative solutions. Negotiation itself, after all, can be a part of apprenticing.

Among all of these specific strategies is an important ideal: the remaking of a relationship with a child the parent has known for so many years. As they do with a newborn, parents must learn ways to delight in their child in this new phase. Now it will mean welcoming that child in new ways: by welcoming her interests, by welcoming her friends. It will still carry the same central message, though. It will mean welcoming not only the person she was but the person she is becoming. As former pope Benedict XVI puts it, "If an individual is to accept himself, someone must say to him: 'It is good that you exist'—must say it, not with words, but with that act of the entire being that we call love."[1] If they are to succeed in this new moment of telling children that it is good they exist, parents must find new pathways of humility, empathy, and solidarity.

As they move through this transition, parents may well find that something else is needed: a new commitment to their own flourishing. Parenting teenagers is psychologically demanding in a way that parenting young children is not. It is all but inevitable that parents will find themselves working through new forms of fatigue or anxiety. And even more, they may find that, as their children move out in the world in new ways, they are tempted to put pressure on them to succeed in ways that will validate their own parenting. Put simply, parents of new teens need to be sure that their sense of worth and of well-being is firmly centered on something *other* than what their child does. As they work hard to make room for their children to become the people they were created to be, parents must continue to do that work for themselves as well. The issues addressed in chapter 10 are important through all phases of parenting, but they become important in new ways during the adolescent stage.

The church community can be a great resource for parents during these years. As children seek new independence, the church community is one place they can find mentors and peers beyond their own families. Even more important, the church can welcome children who are moving toward adulthood. In Judaism, at age thirteen a child is welcomed as a "bar (or bat) mitzvah"—a "son (or daughter) of commandment," now an adult member of the community. A traditional celebration marking this occasion often includes a ceremony in a synagogue and parties. In the Catholic church and in some Protestant traditions, confirmation—a completion of the initiation begun in baptism—functions in a somewhat similar way, although it is not essentially a coming-of-age rite. Together, Christian communities can look for ways to symbolize that even in early adolescence, children begin their transition into an adult world.

Many options exist. Churches could organize a retreat for young teens, together with one or both of their parents, culminating in a moment in which they are welcomed into the adult community. A ceremony of blessing could be planned for a Sunday morning near a child's thirteenth birthday, followed by a celebration. A trip could be planned, perhaps a pilgrimage of sorts to an important site. What will really solidify a moment as a coming-of-age moment, however, is finding ways to invite young teens to real responsibility. Even young teens can take on many crucial jobs: ushering, assisting with music, helping with childcare, participating in service and outreach, reading Scripture or otherwise leading in worship, and more. In our parish, there is always one young person who sits on the parish council and is thus involved in discussions about every aspect of parish life.

Too often, rather than inviting young teens into adult membership, we move them into a youth group where they will be sequestered for four to seven years. It is certainly possible to have a group of young people who gather for fellowship, formation, and service. It is important, however, that such a group also be connected to the larger parish in integral ways, and that the young people involved do not come to see themselves simply as the recipients of a service. As children enter adolescence, it is new forms of apprenticeship—with the slow, attentive mentoring that apprenticeship involves—that will allow them to continue to grow. This period that can be so challenging can also be one of rich opportunity.

Parents and Marriage

In the US—although the numbers have decreased—it is still the case that most parents living with children are married.[1] For most, the marriage and the parenting are deeply intertwined, as children are created precisely through the physical intimacy the parents share. We could even say that for adoptive parents, there is a sense in which a sort of overflow of the love they have for one another leads them to open their home to children as well. In the Christian tradition, of course, marriage is much more than physical union. It is a sort of spiritual, emotional, whole-person union that mirrors the one between God and the church. The hospitality offered to children that comes out of that union is not something separate from the marriage but something deeply connected to it.

Yet living out the realities of marriage and of parenting at the same time is not always easy. My husband's and my twentieth wedding anniversary comes immediately to mind. It was summertime, and we were visiting extended family in another state. My husband left home later than I did, as he delayed his departure in order to allow one of our children to attend a could-not-miss event. Then an emergency with another of our children required that I leave suddenly, heading to another location much sooner than I had planned. On the day of our anniversary, my husband arrived in the early-morning hours, after I was asleep. I woke early in order to leave, and although I was glad to see that he had arrived safely, I decided to let him sleep and left without even saying goodbye. We had thought we would get away for an anniversary dinner that evening, but that was not to be. It seemed symbolic of a larger reality: our children's needs often took a large part of our time and energy, and our own plans were often subject to change. We were united in our dedication to our children, and we agreed that the commitments keeping us from our celebration dinner were important. In the busy days that followed, however, we never did make that dinner up.

In order to make sense of the issue as a whole, it will help to consider briefly what marriage *is* in our cultural context—and how it works. Many of the fundamentals come from ancient Christian traditions: ideals, for example, of monogamy and fidelity. In other ways, modern marriages have come to embody much more. A spouse is ideally pictured as a confidant, soul mate, and best friend. Spouses expect more from one another than they have in the past. The isolation of nuclear families discussed in chapter 3 further stretches the marriage and the individuals in it. Spouses often have fewer adult family members close to them, and so they must rely on each other more in every way, for everything from practical to emotional needs. In a sense, then, we ask more of marriage. At the same time, these marriages are themselves less supported by a surrounding community. If and when spouses have a conflict, however, it can be a great gift to have a "village" in which they will find a listening ear and a commitment to confidentiality. And if grandparents are close by, spouses are much more likely to find eager babysitters so that they can get away for an evening or a weekend.

It is good for spouses to begin with the same realization about marriage that I have suggested about parenting: they should acknowledge the reality that they are asked to accomplish a lot, and often without the resources that are really needed. The first step, practically speaking, is simply to be gentle and forgiving with themselves and with each other.

The second step is to find the village that is so needed. This is no easy task for individual couples. Below I will say more about how the church community can step forward and play a part. What married couples *can* do is to recognize this need and place it at the top of their own list of priorities as they make decisions about where and how they will live. It is good to find a house with a large backyard, but it may be even more important to live in proximity to a church community that will anchor the couple and the family.

In the late 1970s, I had an experience that has deeply affected my own thinking on this question. I was part of a youth choir that visited Jesus People USA in Chicago, a large intentional Christian community coming out of the "Jesus movement" that had emerged a few years earlier (the community is still there today!). As we stood in the main meeting room, we learned that all married couples took part in regular conversations that dealt with the reality of their marriages. In that context, where people were able to come to know one another and establish significant levels of trust, couples discussed very direct questions: "What is going well in your marriage right now" "What is hard?" "How can we support you?" I was struck immediately by the sharp contrast with the wall of silence that I knew often surrounded marriages. I was reminded of situations in which conflict or even abuse was carefully hidden from the larger community until a full-blown crisis made it public. There are dangers in the other direction, of course: intentional communities and even individual churches can sometimes fail to respect a couple's privacy or autonomy (particularly in the case of domineering, charismatic leaders). Yet experience made completely clear to me a central truth: marriages, and particularly Christian marriages, are not meant to function in isolation.

Beyond the question of community, there is also work for married couples to do on their own, as they navigate the two-pronged vocation of parenting and marriage. In one sense, marriage has to be nurtured *apart from* parenting. In another sense, marriage has to be nurtured *within* parenting.

First, marriage has to be nurtured apart from parenting. For married parents, marriage and parenting are never fully separated from one another, and yet there is also a way in which the marriage has a kind of priority. This is usually true chronologically, but even more important, it is true in a spiritual and psychological sense. It is important that parents collaborate closely, and that children know that their commitment to one another is solid. The commitment spouses have to one another is the foundation from which commitment to the children grows, and each spouse must be able to trust that their partner will honor that priority.

One implication is that spouses must give their marriage consideration—including time, effort, and other resources—in its own right. Married parents will inevitably give significant amounts of time to planning and negotiating with connection to parenting. I'll say more about this below. Parents must also carve out time and energy to spend more directly on one another. For many couples, this will mean a date night—but that is a tradition that can take many forms. For my husband and me, a weekly plan to leave the kids and go out to dinner was simply impossible for most of our marriage. Childcare was expensive, and we had no family nearby. Nor could we have budgeted for a weekly dinner out. This is a place to be creative, and there are other options for finding time alone together:

- If a weekly date night is not possible, a monthly tradition may be more doable.

- If weekend evenings are too difficult, there may be ways for a married couple to find time together during the day.

- If childcare is more available in longer stretches, couples may organize their time in a different way. We have, for example, traveled to visit our children's grandparents and then planned for an evening or an overnight away while there.

- If a full dinner out is not in the budget, there may be simpler possibilities, such as a date for coffee or ice cream.

- In one community where we lived, I knew three young couples who had a "date night club." For the first three Saturdays of each month, one couple would provide childcare for all of the children, and the other two couples would go out. They each were able to go out twice a month, and the couple providing childcare often looked forward to planning meals and activities. (The kids loved "date night club" as much as their parents did!)

- For some couples, a date night at home may actually make most sense. I once knew a couple with five young children whose budget was extremely tight. On Saturdays they planned very busy, outdoor days for the kids and then put them to bed a half-hour early. Then they made a favorite Tex-Mex meal together and celebrated with a glass of a very simple cocktail: lime juice, sugar, water, and a dash of tequila. It cost almost nothing, but it was something they both looked forward to, and it became a ritual over many years.

Second, marriage has to be nurtured *within* parenting. As important as it may be for parents to find time for themselves, it is also true that married parents will mostly live their marriage closely tied to, rather than apart from, their parenting work. What might it look like to thrive in that situation?

First, spouses can express regular gratitude for the work their partner does in their shared vocation of raising children. It is good to express that gratitude regularly, but even more fundamental is the simple habit of *noticing* with gratitude the contributions that a spouse is making. The contributions that could be taken account of are many and varied: direct supervision of children, financial support, planning and carrying out the many details involved in children's care, as well as less tangible gifts like patience, kindness, and humor. To reorient toward gratitude in this way may seem like a small thing, but it can reframe the whole reality of shared parenthood.

Gratitude of this kind can be directed not only to your spouse but, just as importantly, to God. This simple practice opens up a whole dimension of parenting together that can be overlooked. Spouses rely on one another, but they also rely on God. In an ultimate sense, it is God who supplies everything they need, and in a very real and intimate sense, God is present with them and in them as they move through the challenges and blessings of each day.

Second, spouses can commit to supporting one another in practical ways. Above all, they can be vigilant in kindness. Whether this means speaking respectfully or refilling a tank with gas or offering a much-needed cup of coffee, these small acts add up to a vast difference over time. Being considerate of one another applies in particular ways when spouses are parenting together. Although it can be very difficult, spouses can try to give one another space in parenting. They can commit to avoid criticizing one another in front of their children.

(For this, both the spouse *and* the children will likely be grateful!) This is not to say that every criticism should be brushed under the rug or that children should never be made aware of their parents' differences. It is to say that these matters are to be handled with care.

Third, spouses can look for ways to give one another time and space for life-giving forms of rest and recreation away from family responsibilities. Especially when life is demanding, this is not easy (wives who are frustrated with their husbands spending time with buddies is a well-worn trope). And yet this form of desiring the flourishing of the other is a profound form of solidarity. The heart of this ideal is spouses who are committed to one another both as partners and as co-parents.

Fourth, particularly in light of the goals described above, spouses can support one another by exercising patience when they fall short. This can be challenging. A great deal is at stake in parenting, and sometimes parents simply feel strongly that a spouse is coming at the task in a wrongheaded way. Parenting with a partner means choosing forgiveness and looking for ways to address differences respectfully.

Finally, knowing that coordinating their efforts is a big job, spouses can make a point of giving time to the conversations and planning that are needed to parent together. In chapter 5 we talked about the central idea of parenting as apprenticeship. One foundational conversation might begin by considering central questions related to that model: "Are our lives organized in a way that allows for fruitful apprenticeship?" "What exactly are we apprenticing our children to?" The possibilities for conversation will vary in different families and different seasons. Some couples are able to plan a yearly retreat where they ask these kinds of questions. My husband and I have often followed a practice of two weekly conversations: one focused on catching up with one another and one on the practicalities of parenting. At one particularly demanding moment, we sat down together daily to take stock of the situation and to ask ourselves what we needed to do next.

If they are integrated in these kinds of ways, parenting and marriage are two callings that can come together, each enriching the other. In this light, we perhaps should avoid speaking of a couple's time away together as "taking time for your marriage." A candlelit dinner is part of a marriage, but so is tending to a sick child in the middle of the night. Not only can marriage enrich parenting, but parenting together can also enrich marriage. The combination can be complicated, but it can also be fruitful and rich.

Before leaving the topic, I want to say a brief word about certain situations in which marriage and parenting are even more distinct from one another. In blended families, for example, you may have a parent and a stepparent. Here, working out parenting in the midst of marriage requires even more careful attention. And even in the case of a divorce, divorced spouses who are co-parenting must still take on many of the same tasks of management. These cases can be more complicated, but these parents need many of the same things that all married parents need: community support, time for conversation and connection, and a commitment to be kind.

Community support for married parents can come from many places, but none is more important than the church community. Many of the possibilities mentioned in other chapters will be relevant here: bringing parents together to discuss discipline or challenges with technology, for example. In the case of married parents, other possibilities appear. Church communities can offer opportunities for couples to attend events with childcare provided, with the goal of either focusing on marriage or just spending time together. Longer events, such as retreats, can be another way to meet these goals, especially as a number of faith-based organizations offer weekend retreats focused on strengthening marriages.

It is true that a life of marriage and parenting is one that brings many challenges. If parents have the resources and options they need, however, this is also a life that can be overflowing with the richest of blessings.

14

Single Parents

I have never been a single parent. The closest I have come is the experience of solo parenting while my husband was out of town, sometimes overseas, for a couple weeks. I suddenly found myself on my own to manage everything: cooking, cleaning, homework, kids' activities, as well as the random trip to the ER that always seemed to fall during those times. By the time my husband returned home, I had arrived at two convictions. First, it was not so much the quantity of things to be accomplished that affected me over that time as it was the stark sense that I was on my own, that the responsibility fell completely on my shoulders. Second, I became convinced that my temporary state of single parenting was nothing but a faint echo of what single parents actually take on over the course of many years.

On the one hand, everything we have said about parents in the book is simply magnified for single parents. If all parents need a supportive village around them, then single parents need one even more so. If all parents need to choose simplicity carefully and intentionally, then this is even more true for single parents. Keeping up with discipline or with challenges related to technology use can be even more demanding for single parents. On the other hand, several things can be said specifically about the challenge of solo parenting.

First, although it is not true for all single parents, many will be navigating a relationship with a former partner and co-parent. In many cases, this brings unprecedented kinds of stress. Negotiations related to custody, childcare payments, visitation, as well as many decisions about parenting, can leave single parents depleted and demoralized—at the same time that day-to-day parenting takes up most of their energy.

Second, finances can be of special concern to single parents. With the added cost of dependents but without a partner who might also generate income or stay at home to help the whole family economize, margins are tight in a single-parent household. This is especially true in the case of job loss or other economic pressures.

Finally, single parents face a wide-ranging experience of simply having no one to fall back on in day-to-day family life. These specific challenges come together to create a unique sense of responsibility and often strain. This phenomenon is not easy to pinpoint or to categorize, but single parents will recognize it well.

In the face of all these challenges, the most important thing for faith communities and community leaders to know is that single parents need support. They need the same support that other parents need: opportunities to connect and collaborate with other parents in forms of solidarity, help with childcare that allows them to be present at these and other conversations, and the opportunity to give their opinions as churches create community life. There are also further ways to support single parents in particular. Single parents need people who will

- volunteer to watch their children. Especially for single parents who have no extended family nearby, this can be a huge gift. It may be the only way for them to go out to do errands, socialize, or just to relax.

- volunteer to watch their children at their own house. This gives single parents the rare luxury of time at home without their children. Let them stay in!

- bring meals. Even better is bringing a meal on a regular basis—at least for some period of time. Dinner on one weeknight will allow a harried single parent a little more time for all the things that must be accomplished, from homework to bath time.

- consider single parents first when they have hand-me-down clothing or toys. Again, you have to be tactful about how you offer hand-me-downs, but most single parents will appreciate the gesture, even if their kids' bookshelves and toy boxes are overflowing. Maybe you can take a few of their old ones and donate them to a library or thrift store.

- volunteer to help with errands. Parents can double up on errands they are already running for their own families, buying school supplies or picking up children from an activity. Anyone can offer to help with items needed at the grocery store or drugstore.

- offer to be a back-up person at school. Schools always need a name and a phone number as an emergency contact. And single parents often need someone to help out when the school announces an early dismissal. Fellow parents who have children at the same school would be a natural fit here.

- help with house or lawn maintenance. Especially when there are larger jobs such as raking leaves or shoveling snow, single parents are likely to appreciate a hand.

- reach out on holidays and special occasions. Offer childcare specifically to allow single parents to do Christmas shopping or to go out trick-or-treating with an older child—even though they may have a baby who needs to be in bed. A single dad will likely appreciate an offer to help with hair or makeup or photography for his daughter's prom. A single mom will likely appreciate a friend stopping by with flowers for Valentine's Day or Mother's Day.

Ultimately, the best way to help a single parent with these many practical details is to listen and to be available. Single parents know what they need most, and if they have a phone number they know they can call, they will. Church communities may want to organize, formally or informally, ways that certain individuals or families can connect personally with single parents, build a real friendship, and come to understand what they need most over time.

This can often be accomplished best when particular individuals or families step up to accompany particular single parents. A married couple with children of similar ages, or perhaps attending the same school, will have certain practical advantages. A young, single person will have other ways to be present, perhaps especially in availability. An older couple can step in, bringing their own experience as parents and also, perhaps, the greater availability and slower pace of retirement. These are the kind of relationship that allow a real friendship to take root. As much as single parents need practical assistance of many kinds, they also need people who will simply make the extra effort to connect and walk with them, to build real and lasting relationships.

Churches can offer their own forms of support. They can facilitate, where possible, the kinds of friendships mentioned above. Where they celebrate and support married couples, they can keep single parents in mind, looking for ways to include them. Providing childcare for events is often essential in order for single parents to attend. A high school or young adult ministry might even focus on single parents by hosting a single parents' day out, where they provide childcare specifically for these families. Churches have the possibility of bringing single parents together, perhaps by starting a single-parent support group or creating an online support group that is specific to single moms. Assisting with financial needs must be done with discretion, but here a local church can leverage the whole community. Members of the church can be given the opportunity to donate appliances, children's clothes, toys, or furniture, and the church can organize distribution to those who need them.

Finally, in addition to care from the community, single parents can be reminded and encouraged to care for themselves, even while they are caring for their children. (This is a message that will benefit all parents!) Even with good intentions, churches sometimes speak of the sacrifices that parents must make or the hardships involved. Alongside those messages, it is important also to speak about the way that holiness and wholeness are linked and that practices of care for ourselves are part of the Christian life: eating well, taking time to exercise, keeping in touch with friends, getting enough rest, and, when needed, seeking professional counseling to support mental health.

The challenges are certainly significant, but we will go wrong if we think of single parents only in terms of the needs they have. Especially as they receive the support they need, single parents can be a profound gift to their communities. I think of one fellow adoptive mom I have come to know. She is a nurse who has significant experience with trauma and emotional challenge, and she has brought all that to bear in raising the three boys she has adopted (all of whom came to her as older children). There have been very hard moments for her along the way, especially after her mother unexpectedly passed away, but she has also found ways to support others, including running an online support group for adoptive moms and sharing her own hard-won wisdom. She has many gifts to offer, and finding the support she needs has freed her up to do that.

For me, it has been striking to see adoptive families where single parents can actually offer strengths that married parents cannot. Some children with challenges in attachment find it very difficult to live in two-parent families. Navigating with two authority-figure caregivers is just too anxiety-producing for them. When they have only one parent, they can relax and focus and move toward the healing they need. Perhaps this example can help us avoid seeing single parents only as a plan B. God has purposes to work out with every family, every parent, and every child. Single parents can be part of bringing those purposes to fruition.

Maybe the family of Jesus is one example of this. We find no mention of Joseph in the Gospel narratives of Jesus's ministry, and tradition has it that he passed away before those years arrived. Although the Gospel account of Jesus teaching in the temple records Joseph as being present when Jesus was twelve, we have no way of knowing when exactly Joseph's death occurred. We could certainly say that in Mary's most painful moments as a mother, she is alone. At the moments when she most needs her spouse for comfort and support, he is not there. At the very least, this serves as a strong reminder that God is present and at work in and through single parents. Their families too can be families full of love and purpose.

15

School and Other Ways of Learning

Many years ago, I had the opportunity to visit a friend in the hospital very shortly after she gave birth to her first child, a girl. She handed me her tiny new daughter and I cooed and bounced. Then I walked to the window, where a sunset was spreading across the sky. "Welcome to the world," I told her. "It's amazing here."

This is what all parents are called to do. Parents welcome their children to the world and invite them to consider it with curiosity and wonder; to employ their innate skills of observation, analysis, and imagination; and then to respond, whether in conversation, writing, building, the arts, or some other way. They hand on the traditions in which those before them have found beauty, insight, and wisdom. "Education," said G. K. Chesterton, "is simply the soul of a society as it passes from one generation to another."[1]

Sometimes this process is pursued—especially in certain ways and in regard to certain subjects—at a place we call "school." It is important to see school in its context. The modern school system was founded less than two hundred years ago. Even then, it was another one hundred years before school attendance became widespread (and even longer until it was mandatory throughout the US). Until the early twentieth century, most children in the US who attended school went to a one-teacher, one-room schoolhouse for first through eighth grade. Children were not usually assigned to a grade level, and their lessons might be corrected, but they did not receive grades. In earlier eras, children of the wealthy might attend boarding schools or receive private tutoring, but most were taught basic academic skills at home or in the context of work apprenticeships.

The goal of the school system familiar to us was standardization and professionalization. As we still see in practices of accreditation and standardized testing, it was hoped that minimum standards would be met for all students, preparing them well to move forward into adulthood. Particularly in the context of a more industrialized and complicated world, it was judged that competency in reading, writing, and mathematics would be required of many more people. History and science—and sometimes studies in the arts or in religion—rounded out a standard course of study. Today, schools continue to evolve, searching for the form best suited to a new millennium.

In some ways, though, if we want to understand school and its relationship to parenting, it is good to remember that school is only one way that parents engage in this process of educating their children (and, if we are honest, school is only a small part of that process for any child). The larger context is the goal of learning, and that can happen anywhere and everywhere. One of the most fulfilling possibilities in moving from a management paradigm of parenting to an apprenticeship paradigm of parenting is that parents can make space for the joy of wondering about the world and exploring it together with their children.

The single most important way for this to happen is conversation. It may sound simple or overly obvious, but in the case of most children, nothing is more nourishing to their young minds than a gentle, consistent, years-long engagement in conversation with parents. This will happen differently at various stages of a child's development. Babies and toddlers are usually keenly ready for this interaction, their minds soaking it in as they lay down the foundations for the rest of their life. The possibilities when parents will lay aside their handheld devices and other distractions and use the moments with their children with love and care are immense. "When we cut the carrot like this, it looks like pennies, doesn't it?" "Does your doll need a plate too?" "Look at this rain! Where do you think it comes from?" Parents will certainly sometimes instruct, but there are a multitude of other options that make this conversation a rich one: "What do you see? Did you notice . . . ? What do you think about . . . ?" A good conversation is like a dance, and usually children will respond with delight when we invite them to join in.

Closely related to this practice of conversation is music, including song and dance. Parents and others who are educating children are sometimes tempted to think of music only as background noise in relation to the task at hand. Music, however, is a kind of miracle for the work of education: it can teach, draw out, console, amaze, invigorate, and foster relationship, sometimes all at the same time. Just listening to music of all kinds can be deeply enriching, but making music, or participating by singing or dancing, brings a new level of engagement and joy.

Reading, and the larger categories of story and narrative, is very close to conversation and music in importance. At present, parents have a remarkable resource: strikingly beautiful children's books are easily available, for purchase and in public libraries. Because repetition of stories has so many advantages for young minds, even a small collection of books, read over and over again, has the potential for immense benefit. When a habit like this takes hold, it can also be maintained for longer than we sometimes think. In our family, we developed a habit of reading books aloud long after our children began to be able to read themselves. Our oldest son recently let my husband and me know that one of his favorite memories from his growing-up years is reading a work of historical fiction set in ancient Rome. He and his younger brother were moving toward the end of their elementary years at that time.

Recently in our own home, my father-in-law, now over eighty, was visiting. After a rousing game of cards, one of our sons asked him what sorts of activities he did with his family when he was growing up. What followed was more than an hour of stories, one after the other, offering a glimpse of a world that is gone now and also of the people involved: my children's grandparents, great-grandparents, and great-great-grandparents, and their own stories, including joys, tragedies, and wise and foolish decisions along the way. Hearing the stories of their grandmother, who moved from the city to marry the farmer she had fallen in love with, and their grandfather, who fell gravely ill in his twenties and had to rethink his whole life, gave our children specific ways to understand and engage with the world that cannot be replaced by anything else. If we imagine parenting as mapmaking, then telling stories such as these is a way to offer a map.

Finally, if we are thinking about the very foundations of education, we have to include the whole realm of engagement in the world with our bodies. Dancing at a wedding, hiking in the woods, walking long city blocks, or measuring ingredients to bake a cake: these can all be components in a rich education, especially when they are undertaken in the context of conversation described above. In our own cultural setting, where learning is often imagined as happening while a child is seated at a desk, it is good to be reminded that using our bodies with energy and purpose is not best understood simply as a break from "real learning"; it is learning itself. For some children it is particularly crucial.

Learning has to be built on these foundations.

As we put these sorts of learning together, it is also good to recall the largest horizon of all for parents of faith. Learning is not simply a neutral encounter with facts; it is part of the largest task of all: learning to love. The moment when children learn about the various jobs and roles that are part of society is the best moment to learn also that we regard every person as possessing profound innate dignity, as someone to whom we owe gratitude. And if we remember what Deuteronomy 6:5 calls the first commandment (also later reiterated by Jesus to his followers)—"You shall love the LORD, your God, with your whole heart, and with your whole being, and with your whole strength"—a whole world opens up. Solving the most abstract math problem can become a way of loving God, the author of order and elegance.

With all this in mind, we can turn to the questions that arise about where and how this learning will happen for children, questions that become particularly acute as they become capable of more complex and abstract thought and as their education accordingly becomes more sophisticated. School is the answer for most children. In this case, parents, who are always the primary educators of their children in the largest sense, entrust their children to those with specific training and expertise. At the same time, they partner with their children's teachers, encouraging children to meet the expectations that they encounter in a school context.

The specific school setting can vary tremendously. In our own family, we have sent children to public and private schools, large and small, in a wide variety of settings. Our oldest daughter began preschool when she was three in a small church-related school a short walk from home. Our oldest son completed his high school education in a large public inner-city high school, a school drawing students from many different economic, racial, and cultural backgrounds. There were many decisions to be made about schooling, and they were not always easy ones.

We always began with the fundamentals above clearly in view: Where could we send our children to learn in the fullest way? Where would they be treated as "whole persons"? Where would they find teachers and conversation partners who would recognize that we never simply learn "bare facts" about the world but are always learning about the world as a whole and our place in it?

We looked for schools that would recognize the magnitude and privilege of being invited in as partners with us, our children's parents. We hoped for schools that themselves involved a real sense of community and connection, and that prioritized inviting parents in as a part of that community. We valued attachment to our children, and we were looking for what authors Gordon Neufeld and Gabor Maté call an "attachment village."[2]

In Providence, the primary place our children grew up, our neighborhood parish school had real advantages in this way for our family. The school building was visible from our living room window, and children up and down our street were classmates and friends, as well as neighbors. When the church bell sounded, announcing that school would begin in five minutes, latecomers still had time—if they hurry!—to avoid being marked late. When I heard stories about old-fashioned neighborhoods, where children roamed the streets and moved from one house to another under the watchful eyes of various parents, it sounded very familiar. I realized that those watchful eyes were not simply about catching kids getting into trouble but also about communicating to them that the attachment village was at work and that they were surrounded by a sort of net of communal connection. This is not to say that correction of other people's children was not sometimes involved. I remember the day that one of our children went missing just after school, and we actually got to the moment where the school principal and I were standing in her office, about to phone the police. Our son was happily and quietly playing LEGOs in the upstairs bedroom of a nearby home, and the older sibling in charge had not realized that he had walked in. As it happened, a fellow parent spoke with my son before I did, and he wisely instructed him in the intricacies involved: "When your mom sees you, she is going to be very happy, and then she might also be mad. It would be good for you to tell her that, in the future, you will let her know where you are." On another occasion, one of our sons used chalk to write something less-than-appropriate on the school blacktop. Another father said one of the most helpful things he possibly could have said: "You are better than this."

In the goal of finding this kind of community, parents have many possibilities. Parents who have the room in their schedules can lean in with the goal of creating community at the schools their children attend. Becoming involved themselves as volunteers enables their getting to know both their children's teachers and the parents of other children. Throughout my own early school years, my father, who often traveled for work, also had days off during the week, and he made a habit of coming to eat lunch with me at school occasionally. It was unusual even then, but the message to me was evident: "I have your back." For parents who are able to do this, it can be a fruitful way forward. Parents with less time and fewer resources can do what they can with electronic communication and really leaning into connection with their children. The crucial thing is to let children know that they are not being sent off to fend for themselves.

Given all these factors, it is no accident that faith communities have so often founded schools. In some cases, it has been to prevent children from contact with influences their parents were concerned about, but there is a positive goal as well: the possibility of a high level of integration, both for the child personally and with the child's parents. A school with faith at its center can address a child in a way that includes intellectual, emotional, and spiritual elements. If its faith elements overlap with the commitments of a child's parents, then an important kind of continuity is established between home and school.

There is always a danger with church-related schools. They can become insular, and in some cases there can be less transparency in addressing important challenges that arise. It is also possible to create a faith-based school that is open. Our own family's parish is now home to a high school with a particular and clear mission: to provide a home for students who might have otherwise not had such an education available to them. It is a small school, focusing on building relationships between students and the school's teachers and staff. It does not have all the extras that the best-resourced schools have, but it is committed to meeting students where they are and moving them to confidence and competence in the academic skills that are crucial for a high school diploma. It has taken on the task of significant fundraising both prior to its opening and in an ongoing way, such that students are admitted without regard to their financial status. Each family pays what it can. The school is unapologetically faith-based, but it welcomes any family who is interested in partnering with them in their child's education.

Whether in the way our parish high school does it, or in the context of a large, public school, it is good to note that school is also a way for families to connect to and invest in their larger communities. What makes most sense for children is for parents to find or to build an attachment village, rather than sending children as individual ambassadors from their home to that larger community. Are we meeting the goal of engaging community in other ways?

In some cases, parents will decide that traditional school is not the right choice for their children and will choose instead some form of homeschooling. It requires significant resources in terms of both time and energy, but homeschooling does have real advantages if we are thinking of parenting in terms of apprenticeship, if only for the greater amount of time that parents spend with children. Of course, homeschooling also has its innate challenges. For parents who work full time or who have other significant obligations, balancing these with supervision of, and interaction with, their children is a real question. For some parents, homeschooling is more challenging in the middle school or high school years, when children would benefit from the extracurricular activities or the more specialized instruction that schools can offer. For some parents of students with unusual needs, a well-resourced school offers support that cannot be replicated at home.

For those parents who do consider homeschooling, it is important to remember that homeschooling can include very different structures and plans. Some parents spend virtually all their time with their homeschooled children, only occasionally including an additional activity of one kind or another. Some parents connect their child to homeschooling cooperatives, where parents pool resources and might, for example, meet together twice a week for classes and socializing. Some homeschooled high schoolers are not taught by their parents at all but rely instead on classes taught online or nearby college classes that are open to them.

What all this means is that as they educate their children, whether directly or by delegating to others, parents have a very significant task before them, and many will find a dizzying array of options. Those who want to support them can assist in many ways. Churches and other faith communities, especially, are uniquely important.

As in many other areas, simply bringing parents together for discussion and discernment prevents them from feeling they are alone in these tasks and decisions. Church and other faith communities can be intentional about creating attachment villages, which will serve families well in whatever decisions they make about education. In some cases, these two practices may be connected to supporting—or even founding—faith-based schools. In other cases, they may result in homeschooling cooperatives or support groups. For students in some school situations, their church community may simply be the place where faith is nurtured, as it is not an explicit part of their school day. Finally, for students who are in a school situation that is lonely or unfriendly, a faith community can provide an indispensable counterbalance, a village where they know they are welcomed and loved.

Many other possibilities exist as well, as communities stand alongside parents and their children. These communities also have an investment, after all. Parents have a primary responsibility to educate their children, but it is the community as a whole that needs a way to pass its soul along.

16

Later Adolescence

We have had teenagers at our house for thirteen years, and our youngest has five years before he leaves the teenage years. It has been a hectic, demanding, and delightful phase. I know that other parents have particular concerns about how to parent older teens because when I write or speak about this phase, they pull me aside to say in hushed tones: "*Those* are the years I'm *really* nervous about." My oldest daughter made me laugh out loud one day when she was in her early twenties and I was briefly describing some hard moments with one of her siblings. "Teenagers!" she said, and shrugged her shoulders. "What are you gonna do?!"

Teenagers certainly can be challenging. In our family, the teenage years have included not only concerns about things like grades and relationships but also bigger worries: picking up one of our children from the local police station, walking through a possible pregnancy, a drug overdose that ended in the hospital, and dropping a child off at a therapeutic, residential treatment program. One of the things that I want most to tell younger parents is that my husband and I have had experiences more difficult than we could have imagined—and we have survived. But even with those hard moments, I also want to remind them of something else: teenagers can be simply remarkable, in big and small ways. During my children's teenage years, I have watched as they have tried new things, conquered their fears, and acquired many skills that surpass my own. One started a jazz band;

another started a business. When one lost a friend to gun violence, he and other friends worked through their grief together in deeply moving ways.

I would also want to tell them this: like all the phases of childhood, there are much more important things going on than just surface behaviors. And there is much more going on for parents than simply responding to those behaviors.

Parents of teenagers, even while they continue in busy day-to-day activities, begin to imagine the fruit of their apprenticing work: they begin to catch glimpses of their child as an adult. These years involve nothing less than a sea change in the focus of parenting work and in parents' own understanding of themselves. For most families, they are years filled with rituals—the first school dance, the acquiring of a driver's license, the last football game, high school graduation. Perhaps these traditions are all needed, not only for the teens themselves but for their parents, precisely because the ground is shifting beneath their feet and this familiar set of events can help them to steady themselves.

Parents of older teenagers have a complex set of transitions to navigate. Above all, the shift begun in early adolescence from directing to responding will ideally accelerate significantly. In a very small number of matters, parents must continue to set clear boundaries and to impose obligations. Even an eighteen-year-old can be expected to let her parents know when she will be home or to take out the trash as part of regular chores. In the vast majority of issues, though—what a child eats, what clothing she wears, whom she chooses as friends— parents are now consultants rather than supervisors. For me, this has been reflected in a concrete way in my prayers for my children. For many years, I prayed for specific things: "Give my daughter a sturdy sense of her own self-worth." "Lead my son through this dark circumstance in which he finds himself." When they reached their later adolescent years, I found that my prayers shifted. In truth, I felt less and less sure about what was the best thing. Success in this venture? Or the insights that could come with failure? The end of this relationship? Or its transformation into something richer? Over time, I found that all my prayers were condensed into one: "Lord, give my child whatever she needs most. Whatever courage, whatever consolation, whatever encouragement, whatever challenge. Whatever she needs most." For me, this became a central practice in my children's last transition to adulthood.

At least two things about this process are especially difficult. The first is to know exactly when and how to relinquish control. When is a teenager ready to stay at home alone while parents travel? What should parents do when they have serious concerns about a girlfriend or boyfriend? Where must parents simply say no to a proposed activity because they feel the risks involved are too great? As parents already know only too well, no handbook exists that will answer all these questions. And even when an answer becomes clear in connection with a particular child, the answer for another child may well be different. Parents and their children often disagree about where these boundaries lie, so there is conflict to navigate and hard conversations to be had.

The second difficulty involved has to do with just how hard it is to step back. Parents feel strongly that they can see better and further than their teenagers, that they know better the consequences that may follow particular decisions—and often they are right. The stakes are high: this is the life of their beloved child. And there are the deeply rooted, long-practiced habits of protecting and directing.

None of this, of course, makes much sense to teenagers. They are very aware of their growing competence: intellectual, physical, and otherwise. Like younger adolescents, they are generally more highly motivated to seek novelty and reward than are adults. Above all, they are ready to make their own decisions about what is best for them.

Several things are crucial for parents at this moment to keep in view (even when it is not easy to do so!). First, the risk that a child will make bad decisions cannot be avoided if children are to become competent and confident adults. To put it negatively: if parents maintain a level of control that prevents any mistakes, they will also make it impossible for their children to build the skills they need. Remembering the lessons of younger childhood can be instructive here. If parents will never let a child climb to a spot where she might fall, she will never really learn to climb.

Second, it is very good to keep in mind that for many older adolescents, a crucial part of charting their course is "trying out" various options and "trying on" various identities. Most of these, especially when adopted suddenly and vehemently, will not constitute a permanent decision. There are some cases where a parent must simply remind themselves that many behaviors appearing in these years are later left far behind.

Third, parents may have to face a difficult truth: In some cases, parental concern and control grow out of the needs of parents as much as the needs of their teenaged children. As they move toward the moment that children will launch into their own adult lives, parents have a tremendous temptation to look for validation of their own parenting in their children's behavior. When children comply with parents' wishes, parents may feel very gratified. High achievement reflects well on parents. There is, of course, nothing wrong with children who turn out well, or with parents feeling proud of them, but parents must be careful that the perception of family and friends is not driving the decisions they make about how they parent their almost-adult children.

Finally, parents of faith must pause and reaffirm to themselves a fundamental truth: God loves their children far more than they ever could. When the time comes to let go, they are not simply sending children into a void and hoping for the best. They are allowing their children to step forward, knowing that, as has always been the case, they will be led and accompanied by the God who created them.

At the same moment that parents let go of so much, they also have new tasks waiting for them. In an important sense, a new person is emerging as a child approaches adulthood, and even parents who have had a rich and warm relationship with their child in the past must now build the foundations of a relationship with this new person. As in the past, the absolute foundation must be unconditional love. As our children entered this phase, and especially as we began to parent children with past trauma, I actually began to say to them explicitly and directly: "There is nothing you can do that will make me love you any less." I began to look for moments in which it would make sense to say explicitly that I could be counted on for support, that my child should never be afraid to speak to me.

These kinds of announcements have their place, but even more important is that parents find tangible ways to communicate to a child, "I am on your side." Near the top of the list is a commitment to continue and expand on the communication style described briefly in chapter 12, in connection with younger adolescents. Reining in their need to correct or to offer their own opinions or perspectives, parents who want to cultivate a rich relationship with their teens must generously include conversational habits that express empathy and openness: really listening, not just to respond but to understand better; reflecting back what has been said by rephrasing and asking for input; asking open-ended questions, especially in the service of better understanding what the teen is saying; expressing compassion directly in whatever way feels most natural to the parent (often something as simple as "That sounds really hard"); and looking for opportunities to offer specific kinds of praise ("That was really thoughtful of you to look out for your brother that way"). Even if it feels a bit awkward, thank the teen for talking. Even if the conversation didn't go exactly as planned, parents' gratitude reveals that connection itself is a great good.

Other practices can help strengthen a parent's relationship with their teen and to establish this sense of solidarity. This is a time to look again for new habits and traditions that allow for connection. When one of our children was an older teen, my husband was able to establish a new tradition that they both really enjoyed: an hour or two spent wandering in a local antiques mall. There is always something new to look at, and it is an ideal way to talk and spend time together in a low-key setting. Parents can also begin sharing their own life experiences in greater detail. Stories that are too difficult to be shared with young children can be shared with older teens and can serve to strengthen the relationship.

One of the many benefits of connecting with older teens is that it can give them an ally as they try to navigate. Not long ago, I was at home in the evening and got a call from one of our older teens. I answered, and her first words to me were, "Are you sure you need me to come home right away?" I paused for a long minute. She continued, "I mean, if it's an emergency, I can come." Suddenly, I realized there was more going on than I could see, and I simply said, "When I need you to come home, I need you to come home." Only later did I learn that she was in a social situation that made her very uncomfortable and she was trying to find her way out of it and back home. When she got home, she thanked me, and I did not require any explanation. Later, she explained everything, and I was glad for both her quick thinking and her sense of confidence that I would be a help to her in that moment.

If we are to talk about the realities of an older teenager's approaching adulthood and the complexities of relationships with parents, we cannot skip over the topic of sexuality. Everything we have said so far is captured with exquisite poignancy as teenagers come to terms with their burgeoning sexuality: their independence, their parents' worries, and the horizon of adulthood not far away. The foundation of conversation described above is essential here: it provides a space of gentleness and trust from which to begin. The possibility that parents will be controlled by fear or will focus on appearances is nowhere more heightened. The need for teens to know that their parents are on their side carries a particular kind of weight. With these dynamics in place, however, it is also true that parents can feel more free to share with their teenagers their own ideals regarding sex, and to create certain limits. In our family, my husband and I have communicated a countercultural set of ideals: sex has its home in marriage, and teenage relationships are happiest and healthiest when sex is not involved. If you hope to limit physical intimacy, you need a set of guidelines in place. We created rules in our own household that sometimes made no sense to our children. Ultimately, we tried to communicate our position as part of a larger context: they could feel confident that, no matter what, we were committed to them.

Another challenging situation, once rare, has now become common: teenagers who are struggling with mental-health challenges, including severe and life-threatening ones. The incidence of anxiety and depression among teens is currently skyrocketing. Seeing their children suffer and withdraw, recognizing that they may even be engaging in self-harm, is uniquely painful and frightening for parents. It is a situation that they almost always feel unequipped to address. Happily, there are also now more resources available than there once were—although finding them and connecting to them can still sometimes be maddeningly difficult. Having weathered a number of mental-health crises in our family, I find myself saying to parents two things, above all. The first is that shame is something to lay aside as quickly and completely as a parent can manage. Shame will creep in to paralyze and to berate. It cannot be of any help. The second is that isolation is untenable. As difficult as it may be, parents in this situation cannot afford not to reach out. Parents need information, they need support, and in a very particular way, they need to have others speak the truth to them: you are beloved, your child is beloved, and you are not alone.

Finally, there is the particular challenge surrounding alcohol and other substances. The temptations for teenagers here are many. Use of alcohol or drugs can soothe fear and anxiety. It is a pathway to socialize more easily in some situations. It feels grown-up, and allows teenagers a sense of the independence and power of adulthood. The worries for parents are just as significant. Put simply, alcohol and drugs can be life-threatening in the worst-case scenario, particularly with teenagers whose still-developing brains are prone to impulsivity. And even when the worst does not happen, these substances can short-circuit the work of social and emotional development that teenagers need to do in these years. When they encounter drug and alcohol use (or even just suspect it), parents often have to work very hard to take the next step: taking a long, deep breath and then connecting with their child in a loving way. Like so many issues for older teens, this requires parents to do two things that may at first seem hard to combine. On the one hand, parents do best if they address the issue very directly with their child, describing concretely the behavior about which they are concerned or the evidence they have encountered. There is usually no need for criticism or chastisement. But parents can and should speak calmly and directly about their concerns. They can also insist on the value of truth-telling if they believe their child is misrepresenting the situation. On the other hand, parents can reaffirm to their child their unconditional love. A situation in which a child has made decisions that the parent disapproves of is precisely an opportunity for the parent to say, "And in this situation too I love you." As with mental-health challenges, parents can also reach out for advice and support. There is no simple blueprint guaranteed to fix the situation, but parents can benefit from the wisdom of many parents who have come before them.

For many parents, these later adolescent years will involve a moment in which their child moves out of their home, temporarily or permanently. This moment can be heavy with emotion, and that is probably because it encapsulates so much of what is happening in this phase of parenting. For many years, parents have taught, encouraged, challenged, and tried to accompany. Then—sometimes very suddenly, it seems—they are required to let go. They are asked to make space for their child to join them in the ranks of "adult" as she becomes the center of her own narrative, and for their family to become only a part of her life. If they can be imagined as running alongside a child who is learning to ride a bike, they are asked to let go. An often-cited quote says that to have a child is to "have your heart go walking around outside your body." That insight takes on new meaning when your heart packs up the car and drives away.

If the demands of parenting described in this chapter seem immense, that is because they are. This can be confusing for parents and invisible to others. Infancy, after all, is assumed to be the really demanding moment of parenthood, or perhaps toddlerhood. And it is true that parents of teenagers do not have to feed their child by hand every few hours, or lie down with the child to get her to nap, or rush to kiss a skinned knee. The emotional, psychological, and relational tasks required—and especially the inner work that is required of parents who want to do them well—are nevertheless enormous, and sometimes overwhelming. In some cases, this is actually the most demanding phase of all. I know more than one parent who worked outside the home when a child was younger but then decided that, given the kind of parental presence needed in their child's teenage years, they would have to either leave their job or find a work-at-home option. This is not the course of events that new parents usually imagine.

Given the immensity of these tasks—and the surprise at that immensity—it is crucial that parents of older teenagers find the support they need. In this phase, mentors who have walked this path before them are especially important. The challenges that can arise are complex, and they require people with experience who will come alongside parents to listen, to advise, and to pray with them. There are ways for church communities to plant the seeds for these sorts of connections—they might sponsor an event focused on "teens and screens," for example—but the real work will be done in the context of connection, relationship, and the sort of conversation that allows for nuance. These private interactions allow parents to share confidential information and thus allow not only for detailed advice but also for trusted conversation partners to celebrate accomplishments and mourn losses that cannot be shared publicly.

At the same time, church communities can come alongside parents by engaging with older teenagers in a particular way. As with all stages of parenting, communities of faith can apprentice children in their own way. Adults who will attend to teenagers, engage them, and live and work alongside them are the single greatest asset that teenagers can have, beyond their own parents. Even more than in early adolescence, older teenagers should be given adult possibilities in church settings. If young people are stretching toward adulthood, adults in their community should be inviting them forward toward that goal. Older teens can do almost all the same sorts of work that adults can, whether serving, leading, or organizing. Older teens often assist in mentoring younger teens and children. Our meal kitchen welcomes volunteers of any age, and teens are often present there. Much of this simply has to do with recognizing all that our teenagers are capable of, and inviting them in.

This last phase of the growing-up years is an intense one, to be sure. Perhaps that is fitting, though. In a sense, it sums up all that has come before. In another sense, it involves that last push before the end of a long effort. For parents, it can be almost like running the last few miles of a marathon: somehow both exhausting and euphoric, and sometimes both at the same time. Those of us who are running and those of us who are cheering are all hoping for the same thing: parents who come to the end of this journey in the same way parents should begin, supported and surrounded by love.

17

Parenting Adults

As children establish their own lives and their own families, it is easy—especially in the setting of modern, Western culture—to imagine that parenting has come to an end. So many of the day-to-day tasks have faded into the past. Changing diapers, giving baths, driving to lessons or practice, monitoring screens: much of these labor-intensive tasks are no longer needed. In reality, though, parenting has not ended so much as it has been transformed.

In this new world, parents are faced with a central task: a radical letting go of the kind of parenting they did for so many years. The truth is that adult children are engaged in the project of their own lives. Especially when freedom and autonomy are so prized, unwanted input from parents can seem like an attempt to prevent their move into full adulthood. If we return to the metaphor of apprenticeship, we could say that adult children have now become masters themselves. Their parents' task is not simply to acknowledge but to celebrate that fact.

This letting go is more difficult than it might seem. As one parent of an adult child said to me recently, "The hardest thing I have ever done as a parent is not saying anything." That difficulty is real, but there are ways to support parents at this crucial moment. We do not always acknowledge how significant this task of letting go is, and we generally offer parents little help in undertaking it successfully.

Over the past several decades, psychologists have increasingly made use of a practice called "life review," a process involving slow and deliberate recollection of past events, positive and negative. Most commonly employed at the end of life, it allows individuals the opportunity to consider and come to terms with the reality of their own story. Typically, they reflect carefully on each phase of their lives. They may direct attention to physical memorabilia or even visit people and places that have been especially important to them. Many report that this kind of intentional reflection on their lives brings a significant sense of peace and a greater readiness to accept the fact that their story is now drawing to a close.

This practice of life review bears interesting similarities to the Ignatian practice of an Examen, introduced in chapter 6. The Examen, developed in the fifteenth century by Ignatius Loyola, is also a habit of thoughtful reflection. This practice is repeated daily and is explicitly prayerful, but its essential character is similar to a life review. Traditionally, the Examen includes five steps: (1) giving thanks for the gifts and blessings of the day; (2) asking for enlightenment, particularly insight into where God has been at work and present in the day; (3) reviewing the events of the day, noting especially what led to "consolation" and what led to "desolation"; (4) seeking forgiveness for times where you have acted, spoken, or thought contrary to God's grace and calling; and (5) resolving to amend faults and to do better the following day.

Taking a life review and the Examen together allows us to imagine a possible practice for parents who have come to the end of their child's growing-up years. A review of this kind would give them the opportunity to reflect deeply on these years, to recall joys, to grieve losses, and to move forward to what will come next. Taking up this task could be done alone, together with a spouse, or with a larger group in which conversations might take place.

This practice could take several forms. Parents might retrace each phase of parenting, moving through the five steps of the Examen for each of them. They could also include elements of a life review, perhaps visiting, for example, the physical locations that were most important in their parenting experience. They could take up specific questions inviting them to reflect on their broad experience of parenting:

• What is the best advice you were ever given as a parent?

• What parenting moments do you treasure most?

- If you could relive one single day as a parent, what day might you choose?
- What do you think you did well as a parent?
- What are the most painful moments for you to recall?
- Where do you think you fell short as a parent?
- What do you most wish had gone differently?
- Where were you most deeply disappointed?
- Where were you most aware of God's presence?
- How was the experience of parenting different from what you expected?
- Is there anything you wish your children knew?
- What advice would you give to new parents?

Answers to these questions might well lead not only to reflection but to action: seeking or granting forgiveness, initiating much-needed conversations, or taking actions of other kinds. This reflection can assist parents simply to absorb more fully how it was that their years of parenting unfolded, celebrating or grieving as they recollect and recognizing more fully how God was present to them along the way.

Offering a practice of this kind would be a great service to parents at the end of a child's growing-up years—and it would also offer a crucial way for them to say goodbye to one form of parenting and move into a new one. Perhaps one reason that parents of adult children can sometimes be overbearing is that they are struggling to move on from their child's growing-up years. They are still trying to get it right or to rewrite the events of those years.

It may seem dramatic to compare the end of parenting to the end of one's life, but treating this transition with seriousness will offer a foundation for moving forward. Ironically, it is only this kind of absorbing and accepting the past that allows for parents to build (once again) a new kind of relationship with their children.

The single biggest change for parents of adults is the call to respect the new boundaries that come along with an adult child's independence. If in the past they had to limit giving their children criticism or unsolicited advice, now parents must simply give it up. Depending on the child and the parent, and the relationship they have built together, it may well happen that adult children seek their parents out for advice or opinion, but where it is not requested, parents can be almost certain that it will be unwelcome. Even solicitous inquiries ("Have you thought about X?" "I hope you will take care of Y.") can easily become the same kind of unwelcome advice in adult children's ears.

Respecting boundaries requires some explicit negotiating of expectations. Whether it is visiting for a college's family weekend or establishing expectations for family holidays, parents of adult children are called on to respect their children's wishes and to be as flexible as they can be. Moving ahead based on assumption, or without respectful consultation, can go quite wrong.

At the same time, parents of adult children do continue to be important in their children's lives. Their support and their judicious praise are invaluable. Even when adult children seem completely independent, a thoughtful word of affirmation from their parents can have a tremendous effect on their sense of self and their sense of confidence. In some cases there are forms of validation that only a parent can offer.

If parents find themselves in the role of grandparent, the need to let go in some ways and to lean in in other ways is only more powerfully present. It is hardly surprising that experienced parents are tempted to share parenting wisdom with their children. It is possible to make gentle suggestions or to offer help; however, parents must be careful that their "help" does not become an unwanted intrusion. At the same time, no one is in a better position to communicate to these young parents, "You are doing a great job."

Drawing back from day-to-day involvement in their children's life also brings a corollary task. Parents must find new ways to move forward in their own lives: to rediscover old interests, to find new ones, to give more time to their spouse or to friends, and to find the places to which God is calling them in the future. As their children move on, parents will find some things fading away: daily and weekly activities, easy connection with other parents, and perhaps most important of all, a sense of being needed. This new season both allows and requires that they turn their attention to their own lives, inner and outer, in a way they may not have done in some time.

With all this said, it is important to note that some adult children will not move quickly to complete independence. In recent years, increasing numbers of young adults have remained in, or returned to, their parents' homes. In part due to economic pressures, and perhaps in part due to other cultural factors, increasing numbers of young adults have found that there are reasons to live with their parents rather than setting up their own households. When this happens, parents face a new set of questions and a new set of challenges. Is having young adults at home a way to create an intergenerational household, with the blessings that togetherness can bring? Is there a "failure to launch" that means young adult children are really not thriving? How can parents tell the difference? And, if they find themselves convinced that their children would be best served by spreading their wings and moving out, what are the strategies and steps they should pursue? These are difficult questions, especially if the parents themselves moved more quickly or more easily to independence.

Parents, of course, must still respect appropriate boundaries with their adult children, but when adult children live at home, it serves as a reminder of something important: boundaries must apply to both parent and child. Just as parents must respect their adult children's limits, so too adult children have limits in what they can expect from their parents. When adult children continue to live at home, everyone involved must navigate the expectations involved. Will the child let the parents know whether she will be home for dinner? Whether she will be sleeping at home? What freedom does she have to entertain guests? Does the child owe rent to her parents? Is she expected to do chores around the house? In the big picture, is this a shared household of adults or the parents' home where their child is a guest?

For many parents, these questions can be resolved successfully, and for some, there is a new phase of living with their child, spending time together, that they never expected. For others, however, such a phase creates significant challenges. Perhaps the most difficult situation of all arises for parents who feel strongly that it is time for an adult child to move on, while their child seems unable or unwilling to do so. A situation like this one can usually be addressed, but parents need support as they do so. It is a profoundly challenging moment, and not one that parents generally prepare for. As with previous stages, parents will need confidants and advisers who can help them work through it with wisdom and love.

Even more painful are situations in which young adult children are truly struggling or making choices that are hard for their parents to watch. When substance abuse or mental illness appears, when adult children are wrestling with unresolved trauma or other serious psychological challenges, it can be intensely difficult. Parents often have little influence, but they may also find that their children turn to them for assistance when thing are not going well. As parents seek to find their way forward, it is essential that they have trusted confidants. It can be very difficult in many cases to know where to draw boundaries, and parents often need the perspective of others who are not as closely connected to the situation in order to find appropriate boundaries.

This final phase of parenting may last a very long time. I recall that when my own grandmother passed away at the age of ninety-six, I realized that she had parented my dad for seventeen years while he lived at home—and then for an additional sixty years after that! This long view is perhaps helpful for parents of younger children to keep in mind. It is easy to become lost in the haze of a child's growing-up days. Certainly those are very important days. But parents can hope that those early days lay the foundation for something even richer and longer lasting: a lifelong relationship. Parenting offers a great honor: the possibility of walking alongside these people who have been given to them to be their children.

In this chapter on parenting adults, it is also helpful to note that people can find themselves thrust into new forms of "parenting" their own aging parents. Recently, a dear friend sat on my couch with tears in her eyes. Her mother is in her eighties and has suddenly become weaker and more frail, but she lives far away. A few months ago she fell in her home, and my friend felt the panic connected to an urgent need. Should she just leave everything and go care for her mom? She managed to navigate that crisis, but now she is facing a longer-term and more difficult dilemma. Her mother needs more help every day, but she is not interested in making the move to live closer to my friend and her family. There is no easy path forward.

Caring for aging parents is complicated. Seeing the person you once knew as strong decline physically and mentally can be a shock. Certain circumstances make the process even more difficult: cases of significant dementia, the need to care for aging parents at a distance, long and difficult experiences of illness, and strained relationships involving unresolved conflict.

Responding to these needs can be overwhelming in itself, but for so many, care for aging parents comes at the same time they are facing the typical demands of parenting their own children. Some will simply reach the limits of their time and energy.

Caring for aging parents is not exactly the same thing as caring for children, but some of the suggestions offered here can help. As they do with their young children, those caring for their parents must learn to see their parents with new eyes, to welcome them, even to delight in them. They must find the community and support they need for the demanding work they are doing. And the suggestions in this chapter are relevant: parenting adults often requires careful navigation and negotiation. When they are "parenting" the adults who once parented them, the complexity often increases. As with every new form of parenting, the possibilities for tenderness are everywhere.

Epilogue

The call to parenting will never be an easy one. To have your heart walk around outside your body means that your heart will be bumped or bruised along the way.

It is not a vocation to be pursued in isolation. What parents need is a network of support, a village. They need a community within which they can have conversations and build friendships and do the important work of discernment they will certainly have to do. Above all, we could say, they need a place where they can rest in a web of rich connection.

As it happens, the possibility of resting in this way is a reality that lies at the very heart of the Christian faith. The God whom Christians worship is above all a God who comes to dwell with us, to delight in us, and to let us know we are loved. This same God invites us to rest in him. When God directs or instructs, it is always with this ultimate good in mind: that we might be able to enjoy what the New Testament describes as "fellowship" with him (1 John 1:3). Growing out of this fellowship is fellowship with one another, a fellowship that ideally is also characterized by rest and delight.

Parenting "experts" will always to be ready to offer parents new tips and tricks: how to get the baby to sleep, how to get dinner on the table in under thirty minutes, how to help a child succeed in school. But parents who are themselves supported by a community will be able to find a focus that is more important than efficiency or productivity, even more important than checking off all the items on their to-do list. They will be able to nurture this fundamental experience of fellowship at the heart of their own families.

In practices of companionship and conversation, solidarity and prayer, this vision of a shared life is lived out. Parenting is hard, but in this parenting model, we see profoundly rich possibility: the chance to share with another person what we know of how to live, to cheer their triumphs and salve their sorrows, to give and receive love, to experience together the big and small moments that make up life. This is a vocation worth giving ourselves to. And for those who walk beside parents, who seek to support them along this path, it asks the best we can give.

Suggested Reading

Arnold, Christoph. *Children's Education in Community: The Basis of Bruderhof Education*. Walden, NY: Plough Publishing House, 1967.

Burns, Jim. *Doing Life with Your Adult Children: Keep Your Mouth Shut and the Welcome Mat Out*. Grand Rapids: Zondervan, 2019.

Connell, Gil, and Cheryl McCarthy. *A Moving Child Is a Learning Child: How the Body Teaches the Brain to Think*. Minneapolis: Free Spirit, 2013.

Delahooke, Mona. *Brain-Body Parenting: How to Stop Managing Behavior and Start Raising Joyful, Resilient Kids*. New York: Harper Wave, 2022.

Dickson, Kim Jocelyn. *The Invisible Toolbox: The Power of Reading to Your Child from Birth to Adolescence*. Coral Gables, FL: Mango Media, 2020.

Doucleff, Michaeleen. *Hunt, Gather, Parent*. New York: Avid Reader, 2022.

Earley, Justin Whitmel. *Habits of the Household: Practicing the Story of God in Everyday Family Rhythms*. Grand Rapids: Zondervan, 2021.

Gopnik, Alison. *The Gardener and the Carpenter: What the New Science of Child Development Tells Us about the Relationship between Parents and Children*. New York: Farrar, Straus & Giroux, 2016.

Hebblethwaite, Margaret. *Motherhood and God*. London: G. Chapman, 1984.

Landry, Bonnie. *Revolution of Mercy: How Kindness Changes Everything*. Scotts Valley, CA: CreateSpace Independent Publishing Platform, 2015.

MacNamara, Deborah. *Rest, Play, Grow: Making Sense of Preschoolers (Or Anyone Who Acts Like One)*. Vancouver: Aona Books, 2016.

Montessori, Maria. *The Discovery of the Child*. Notre Dame, IN: Fides Publishers, 1967.

Neufeld, Gordon, and Gabor Maté. *Hold On to Your Kids: Why Parents Need to Matter More Than Peers*. New York: Random House, 2008.

Peterson, Eugene. *Like Dew Your Youth: Growing Up with Your Teenager.* 2nd ed. Grand Rapids: Eerdmans, 1994.

Siegel, Daniel, and Tina Payne Bryson. *The Power of Showing Up: How Parental Presence Shapes Who Our Kids Become and How Their Brains Get Wired*. New York: Ballantine Books, 2021.

Siegel, Daniel, and Mary Hartzell. *Parenting from the Inside Out: How a Deeper Self-Understanding Can Help You Raise Children Who Thrive*. 10th anniversary ed. New York: Penguin Random House, 2014.

Stephenson, Susan Mayclin, and Silvana Quattrocchi Montanaro. *The Joyful Child: Montessori, Global Wisdom for Birth to Three*. 2nd ed. Arcata, CA: Michael Olaf Montessori Company, 2013.

Notes

Chapter 1 New Parents

1. United States Conference of Catholic Bishops, "Order of Baptism for Several Children," in *The Order of Baptism of Children* (Collegeville, MN: Liturgical Press, 2020), 21n47.

Chapter 2 Beyond Birth

1. Lydia R. Anderson, Paul F. Hemez, and Rose M. Kreider, "Living Arrangements of Children: 2019," Household Economic Studies (United States Census Bureau), 1–20.

2. J. I. Packer, *Knowing God* (Downers Grove, IL: InterVarsity, 1973), 182.

3. To expand a bit more, I would strongly encourage great care around any celebration of Mother's or Father's Day. Not only are many families formed in atypical ways. These holidays also are just hard and ambiguous days for many. There are young women who have just learned that they'll never be able to conceive. There is someone else who just lost his own dad and is only feeling loss on this first Father's Day without him. Another woman may be thinking about the baby she placed for adoption long ago and the empty space in her heart that has never closed. And there are many more.

Chapter 3 Fostering Community, Within and Around

1. This saying exists in many Bantu languages and countries, and in other African traditions and cultures as well. One source to learn more is Mungi Ngomane, *Everyday Ubuntu: Living Better Together, the African Way* (London: Bantam, 2019).

2. See Augustine, *On the Good of Widowhood*, Patrologia Latina 40.450, https://www.newadvent.org/fathers/1311.htm; and Augustine, *Letters* 188.3, Patrologia Latina 33.849, https://www.newadvent.org/fathers/1102188.htm.

3. Dietrich Bonhoeffer, *Life Together*, trans. John W. Doberstein (San Francisco: Harper Collins, 1954), 93.

4. Pope Francis, *Amoris lætitia: Post-synodal Apostolic Exhortation on Love in the Family* (Vatican City: Libreria Editrice Vaticana, 2016), § 28.

Chapter 6 The Growing Years

1. Pope Francis, *Laudato Si'*, The Vatican, May 24, 2015, https://www.vatican.va /content/dam/francesco/pdf/encyclicals/documents/papa-francesco_20150524_enciclica -laudato-si_en.pdf, §213.

Chapter 7 The Art of Discipline

1. John Bosco, quoted in Philip Kosloski, "7 Saintly Tips on How to Discipline a Child, from Don Bosco," *Aleteia*, January 31, 2017, https://aleteia.org/2017/01/31/7-saintly-tips -on-how-to-discipline-a-child/.

Chapter 8 The Challenge of New Technology

1. B. J. Fogg, *Persuasive Technology: Using Computers to Change What We Think and Do* (San Francisco: Morgan Kaufmann, 2002).
2. J. M. Culkin, "A Schoolman's Guide to Marshall McLuhan," *Saturday Review* (1967): 51–53, 71–72.
3. Simone Weil, *Waiting for God* (San Francisco: Harper Perennial, 2009), 57.
4. Weil, *Waiting for God*, 57.

Chapter 10 Parents—and More Than Parents

1. Dr. Harley Rotbart, *No Regrets Parenting: Turning Long Days and Short Years into Cherished Moments with Your Kids* (Kansas City: Andrews McMeel, 2012).

Chapter 12 Moving into Adolescence

1. Benedict XVI, "Address of His Holiness Benedict XVI on the Occasion of Christmas Greetings to the Roman Curia," Clementine Hall, Vatican City, December 22, 2011.

Chapter 13 Parents and Marriage

1. "America's Families and Living Arrangements: 2020," United States Census Bureau, revised November 22, 2021, https://www.census.gov/data/tables/2020/demo/families/cps -2020.html.

Chapter 15 School and Other Ways of Learning

1. G. K. Chesterton, "What Is Called Education?," *The Illustrated London News*, May 7, 1924.
2. Gordon Neufeld and Gabor Maté, *Hold On to Your Kids: Why Parents Need to Matter More Than Peers* (New York: Random House, 2008).

Index